I0828000

PORTLAND'S *HISTORIC* EASTERN CEMETERY

PORTLAND'S *HISTORIC* EASTERN CEMETERY

A Field of Ancient Graves

RON ROMANO

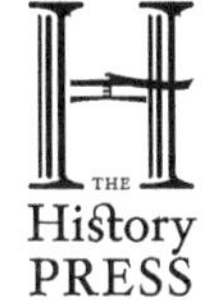

Published by The History Press
Charleston, SC
www.historypress.net

Copyright © 2017 by Ron Romano
All rights reserved

All images are the property of the author unless otherwise noted.
Front cover and back cover, bottom: photos by Holly Doggett.

First published 2017

ISBN 9781540227140

Library of Congress Control Number: 2017945019

Notice: The information in this book is true and complete to the best of our knowledge. It is offered without guarantee on the part of the author or The History Press. The author and The History Press disclaim all liability in connection with the use of this book.

All rights reserved. No part of this book may be reproduced or transmitted in any form whatsoever without prior written permission from the publisher except in the case of brief quotations embodied in critical articles and reviews.

In memory of my father
and
with love to my mother

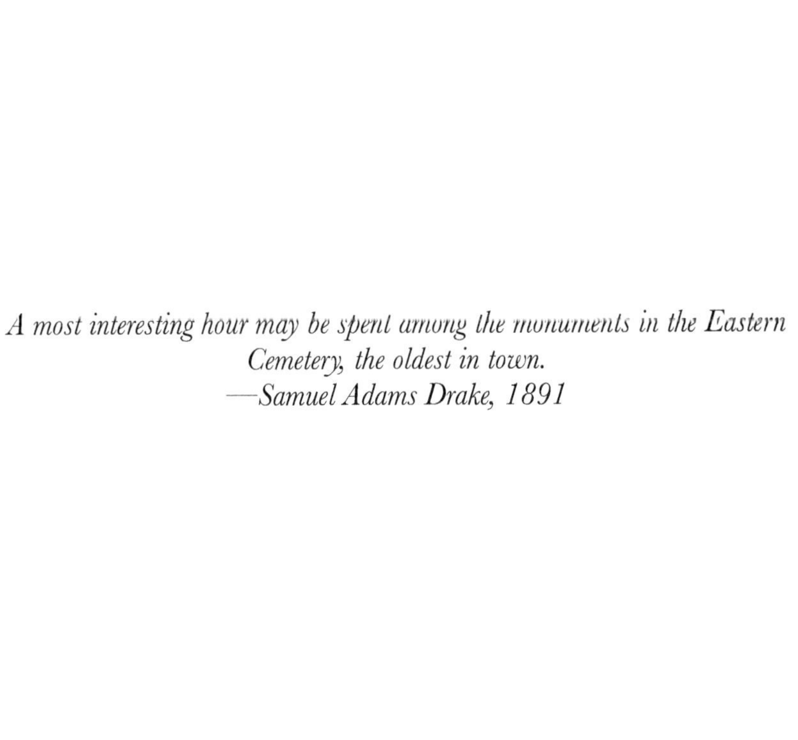

A most interesting hour may be spent among the monuments in the Eastern Cemetery, the oldest in town.

—Samuel Adams Drake, 1891

CONTENTS

ACKNOWLEDGEMENTS

To all my fellow volunteers at Spirits Alive (the nonprofit Friends of Eastern Cemetery), thank you. Four deserve special mention for their contributions to this book: President Janet Alexander (photographs and content advice), chief conservator Martha Zimicki (my beta reader and sounding board), Holly Doggett (sketches and advice) and Diane Brakeley (maps). All deserve a shout-out for their ongoing support: Vana Carmona, Walter Christie, Bill Dalbec, Angela Dexter, Barb Hager, Steve Harding, Corissa Haury, Elena Lippolis, Nikki Meserve, Matt Mueller, Anne Payson, Dave Smith, John Voyer, Pete Weigel, Sarah Whitmore and Alessa Wylie.

Thank you to everyone at Maine Historical Society. I enjoy doing research at the Brown Library, and those visits are always made better by Tiffany Link, Nick Noyes, Jamie Rice and Bill Barry. I also appreciate the help and enthusiastic support received from John Babin, Cindy Murphy, Melissa Spoerl and Sofia Yalouris.

A tip of my hat to MOCA, the Maine Old Cemetery Association; MCMA, the Maine Charitable Mechanic Association; and AGS, the Association for Gravestone Studies. I'm a proud dues-paying member of these organizations and rely on them heavily. Though I've come to know a great many people associated with them, I give special book-related thanks to Perri Black, Jessica Couture, Debi Curry, Art Gaffar, Pat Larrabee, Dennis Montagna, Beth Santore and Cheryl Willis Patten.

Thank you to Joe Dumais, Portland's cemetery superintendent and parks coordinator. While the city owns Eastern Cemetery and is responsible for its upkeep, Joe continues to be a terrific partner to Spirits Alive as we do our spring clean-ups, host visitors on walking tours, trim trees and shrubs and, most importantly, conserve gravestones. His summer park rangers are always helpful. Together, Spirits Alive and the City of Portland are bringing Eastern Cemetery back to life.

To those who offered images or shared their subject expertise with me, thank you: Matt Barker, Mike Daicy, Jim Durbin, Steve Earley, Laurel Gabel, Max Gordon, Andy Grannell, June Hadden Hobbs, Kingsley Itsede, Marilyn Weymouth Seguin and Lenny Telesca.

Finally, thanks to my spouse, family and friends, most of whom understand that I am currently under a spell regarding old gravestones that I can't seem to shake…and many of whom go happily along for the ride.

INTRODUCTION

As leader of the walking tours program for the Friends of Eastern Cemetery (Spirits Alive), I have the honor—and, admittedly, the fun—of creating the script for our volunteer tour guides. Each year, we get better at honing in on what our visitors find most interesting about the historic burial ground and then revising the script to reflect those interests. Walking tours often focus on the famous, but just as interesting to me are the stories of the "regular" people who, for only a day or perhaps a full lifetime, walked the streets of Portland. I start each chapter of this book with a snippet about these regular people whose journeys ended at Eastern Cemetery. Their stories are gleaned from the burial records and are told in just a few sentences, but they help paint a picture of the community at the time they lived, through their occupations, families and ultimately their causes of death.

Eastern Cemetery is a truly unique place: it's the earliest historic landscape in Portland, designated in 1668. It's in the National Register of Historic Places (1973) and received historic cemetery designation by the city in 1990. It's full of interesting stories that reflect more than 350 years of the lives and times of the local people. At rest are seventeenth-century settlers who struggled with the natives over land and resources, eighteenth-century people who had to choose their allegiance either to the king or independence and nineteenth-century abolitionists fighting for the end of slavery.

Two early historians of Portland, William Willis and William Goold, included Eastern Cemetery in their work; I recommend those books for their nineteenth-century consideration of the history of the burial ground. In fact, the subtitle of this book comes from Goold, who in 1886 called the cemetery a "field of ancient graves." The journals kept by Portland's ministers, the Reverends Thomas Smith and Samuel Deane, also provide a fascinating look at everyday life in early Portland. For more modern views, I have three recommendations: Bill Jordan's 1987 *Burial Records, 1717–1962, of the Eastern Cemetery*, a list of interments with some history; the Chicora Foundation's 2011 *Master Plan for Eastern Cemetery*, available on the Spirits Alive website; and my 2016 book, *Early Gravestones in Southern Maine: The Genius of Bartlett Adams.*

I previously published two papers about the cemetery and have drawn from them for this book. "How Many People Are Buried Here?" (published in 2015) is now chapter 13. "Discovery of the Catholic Plots" (published in 2016) is now chapter 10. The full papers are available in the Maine Historical Society's collections for Eastern Cemetery.

A few other notes:

- Eastern Cemetery is located on "Portland Neck," which is the peninsula that consists of the downtown section of today's city. It stretches about three miles from the Eastern Promenade to the Western Promenade and about one mile from Portland Harbor to Back Cove. Before taking the name Portland, this area was known as Falmouth, which today is the town just northeast. I use Neck, peninsula and Portland throughout this book when referring to the area that is, in fact, today's city of Portland.
- On a related note, Maine was a district of Massachusetts until 1820, when it gained statehood. For the purpose of clarity, I refer to Maine and Massachusetts as they exist today—separate states.
- The cemetery has been referred to as the "Burrying" Place, Burying Ground, Common Burying Ground, East Yard, East Cemetery and today's official name, Eastern Cemetery. They are all the same place.

My first book, *Early Gravestones in Southern Maine: The Genius of Bartlett Adams*, told the story of Portland's resident stonecutter, who created a wonderful collection of slate and marble grave markers two hundred years ago, many of which can still be found. This book goes beyond Bartlett, exploring both the history and occupants of the cemetery itself, and includes some new and interesting discoveries. Well covered here are my findings about how some of the minority segments of Portland's population were separated from the majority, even in death.

I love sharing Eastern Cemetery with others, and from that, this book has come to life. I hope you enjoy this armchair tour of a fascinating place and hope that you'll join us on a Spirits Alive guided walk.

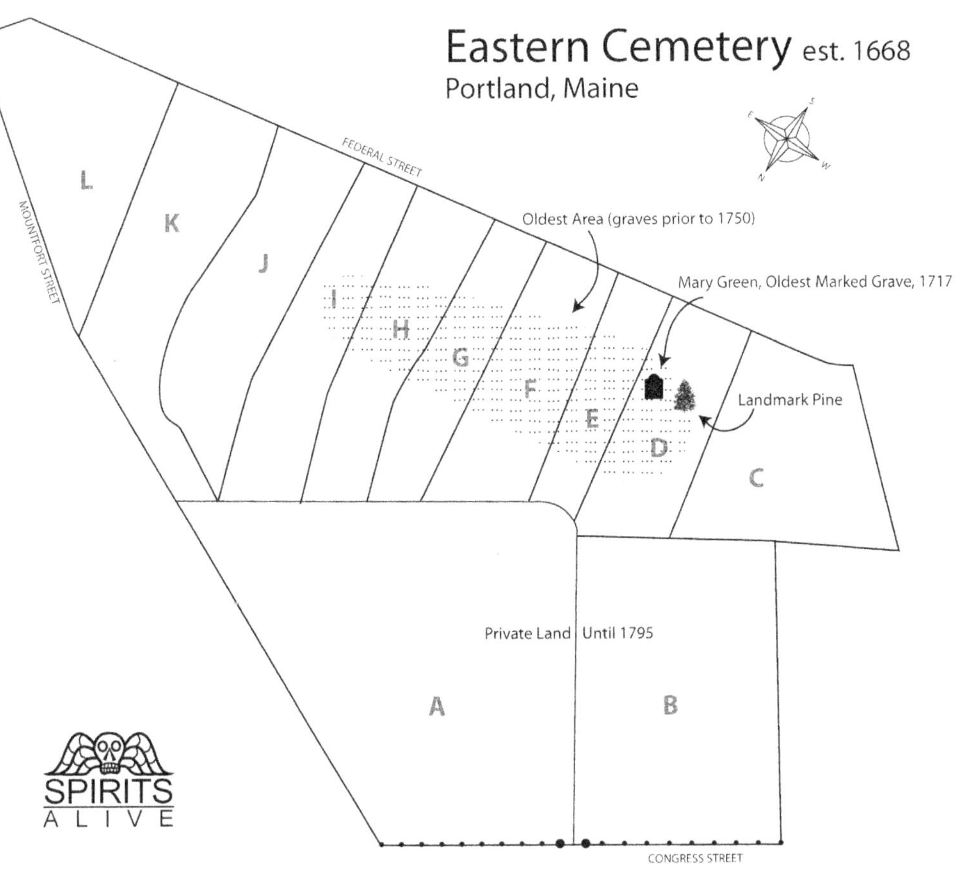

Visitors' map of the six-acre cemetery, with the oldest graves in the shaded area. Section designations A through L were assigned by William Goodwin in 1890. *Courtesy of Diane Brakeley and Spirits Alive.*

Chapter 1

THE BURYING GROUND

Before 1795

The temperature dropped to eight degrees below zero on December 11, 1845. With her husband, John, at sea, Dorcas Lewey braved the frigid temperature and set out alone for an evening of drinking. She was seen at several places around Portland that night. Her body was found the next morning on a pile of snow near their home. Dorcas had frozen to death while intoxicated. She was buried in Eastern Cemetery (her burial record using the surname LaRue), but her plot location is among the many that are unknown.

Most historians agree that the parcel of land serving as the first burying ground for the residents of Portland Neck abutted the homestead lot of first settler George Cleeve (sometimes found as Cleeves). He died around 1668; he and his wife were most likely buried on the hillside upslope from their land. With few structures in the way, the site would have given an unobstructed view of the harbor—even to the open sea. Hillsides were often chosen by settlers to serve as their community burial grounds not for their views but because the land was less suitable for farming. Graves were often left unmarked; settlers were occupied with life, not death. Farming, tending livestock, finding food and fuel and protecting themselves from the natives all took precedence over worrying about a gravestone for a loved one. I've read that at Plymouth Plantation in Massachusetts, the Pilgrims purposely left graves unmarked to prevent the native people from knowing how great the loss of life was in their settlement; the threat of attack was a constant worry.

THE NORWAY PINE

As families began to settle the Neck, some used their own land for burials. But the parcel just north of Cleeve's land became the community burial ground and soon began to fill. The earliest graves are found where an ancient Norway pine grew. It was so tall that it was used as a landmark for ships entering the harbor, and it appears on early maps. The tree blew down during a storm in 1815, and the spot was left bare for some time. In 1865, Willis wrote, "Within the old cemetery stood a large and venerable pine tree…which was a landmark sea-ward for the weather-tossed mariner, and had watched over all the generations who had been buried under its shadow." Willis did not mention that the tree had been replaced between 1815 and 1865, but Goold, in 1886, noted that it had been, for he wrote, "The tree was blown down in about 1815. In later years its site was marked by planting another tree, which flourished until the fire of July, 1866, when the great heat killed it." A white pine planted in 1969 is on the spot today, next to a commemorative boulder.

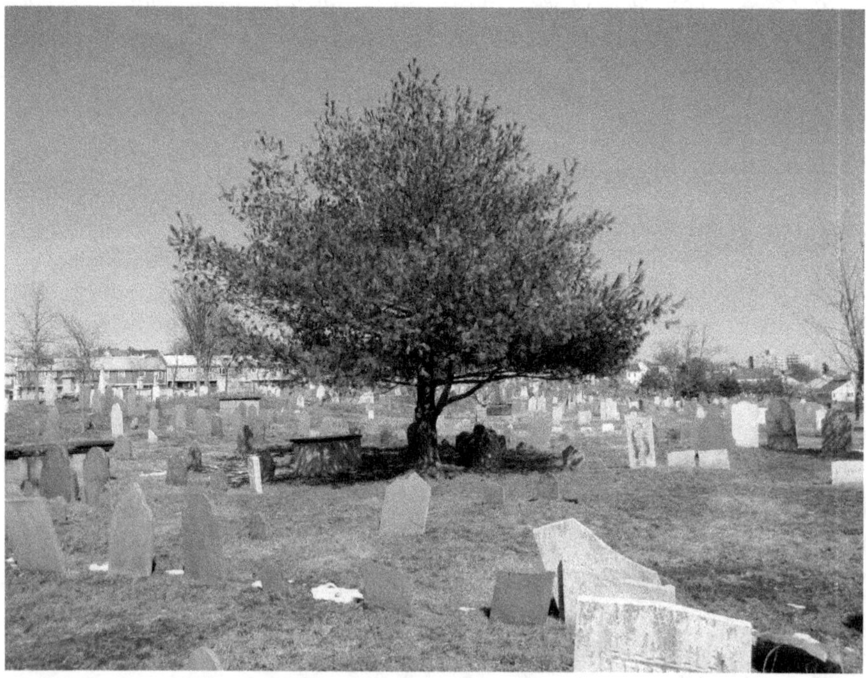

The white pine planted in 1969 on the site of the tall Norway pine that served as a landmark to incoming mariners until 1815. The earliest graves are found nearby.

All agree that this spot was the starting point of the town's burial ground. Graves for twelve men who died in a battle with natives in 1689 are believed to be there. But they may have been the last for a generation, because the conflicts with natives were frequent and harsh. They were not happy that the settlers were taking their land and resources, and who can blame them? Among those killed in the 1689 raid was George Bramhall, who owned four hundred acres of land on what is today the entire west end of the peninsula. His wife and children escaped by sea to Massachusetts; his grandson Cornelius was the first in his line to return.

More than a dozen families resettled Portland in 1713 under the leadership of Major Samuel Moody. Resettlement was successful, and the community began to thrive. With this growth came the need for more burial space, and the Burying Ground pushed its boundaries. The earliest graves and the landmark pine are located in today's Section D (see map). Grave markers for the Major (spelled Moodey, 1729) and his sister-in-law, Mary Green (1717), are just a few steps from the tree. Study of the dates and locations of known burials through the 1750s reveals that when more burial ground was needed, graves were dug to the east (into Sections E through I). By the 1860s, expansion occurred west into Section C. Section designations were not used in those early days; they were assigned by City Engineer William Goodwin when he conducted the first comprehensive cemetery survey in 1890. But they are useful today as we study the cemetery's expansion.

Full Expansion of the Original Ground

Through the end of the 1700s, the Burying Ground expanded eastward to the base of Munjoy Hill, eventually encompassing all of what is now Sections C through L, about 40 percent of today's cemetery area. But problems persisted with this growth. No good record-keeping was in place, and due to the lack of a resident gravestone carver until 1800, few graves were properly marked. When someone died, families could simply bring the body to the cemetery and dig a hole for burial. In fact, families digging graves themselves was a practice that would continue well into the 1830s. A newspaper notice was published in 1840 forbidding people from continuing to do so. Too often when digging graves themselves, they'd find the remains of someone already there. Families ended up being split up; one spouse might be buried in a plot,

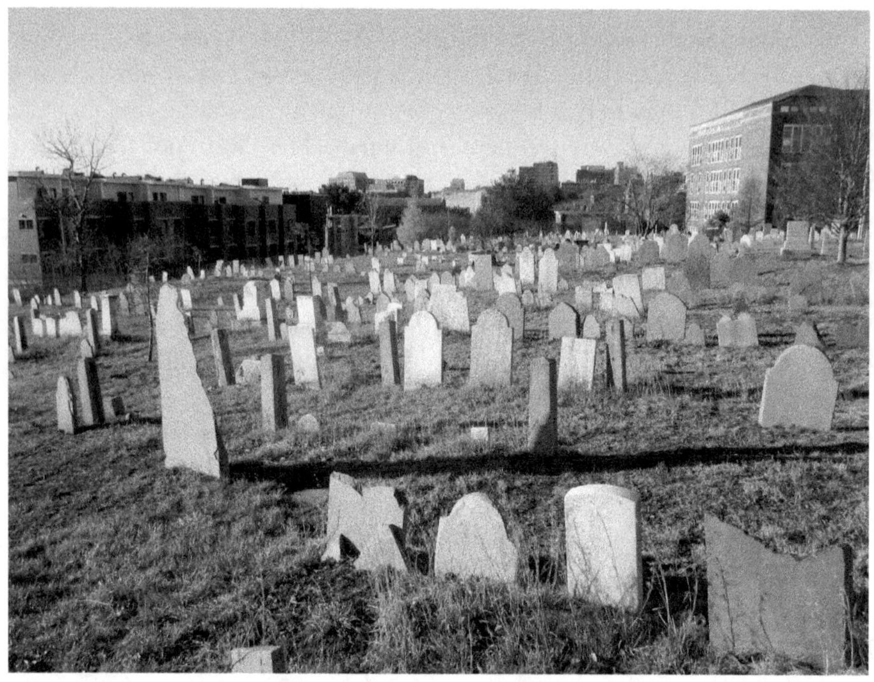

Looking west, only visible are the uninscribed sides of headstones, since bodies were buried head to the west and headstone inscriptions faced away from their graves.

and then with all surrounding space found to be taken by others, the other spouse would end up far away. Mary Martin died in 1822 and was buried in the southeast corner of the cemetery; her husband died in 1836 and was buried in the northeast corner.

Typical burial practices in the eighteenth century consisted of the body being wrapped and tied or sewn into a canvas or woolen cloth shroud. Most would then be placed in a six-sided wooden coffin. Burial was three feet or so below the surface of the ground. Anyone who has visited a colonial burial ground is familiar with the grave depressions and sinkholes that are created over time as the remains of the deceased and their containers deteriorate. The concrete vaults used in today's cemeteries prevent this from happening.

Over 99 percent of the graves at Eastern Cemetery are oriented in an east–west manner. The body was placed head to the west and feet to the east. This has very early roots—the belief was that on judgement day, the resurrected soul would rise to face the dawn. A headstone and footstone (only in common use until about 1850) marked the border of the grave and were placed so that their inscriptions faced away from the plot, allowing visitors to see who was buried there without needing to step on the grave itself. Respect for the dead? Probably. But a more practical reason for not stepping on graves was to avoid falling through as deterioration underground occurred. Few grave depressions still exist in Eastern Cemetery; over the years, they have been filled, and the ground is fairly level. Still, "watch your step" is cautioned on every guided tour.

Underground Tombs

Throughout the old section of the cemetery, multiple graves from one family or another can be found clustered together, evidence that some people claimed family lots. In addition to the open ground used for burials, nine underground tombs were constructed by wealthy families. Jordan suggested that these were built after 1795, when the cemetery more than doubled in size, but I tend to think some of them were put in place before then, as the original part of the cemetery was undergoing its gradual expansion. Underground tombs were not a new concept; they are found in many New England colonial cemeteries and reflect the fact that some prominent families wanted their own private burial space. So it makes sense that underground tombs would have been built prior to 1795. Three members of the Ingraham family died between 1777 and 1783 and are in their Section E family tomb. John Fox and Nathaniel Deering died in 1795 and were buried in their tombs found in Sections F and D, respectively. These interments predate the construction of eighty-six tombs found in Section A, which began around 1798.

Dr. Nathaniel Coffin died in 1766 at age fifty. He'd survived smallpox in 1760 but had failing health thereafter. Reverend Smith wrote in 1763 that the doctor was "breaking and decaying fast" and in 1765 that he had palsy but was continuing to breathe. The burial record for Dr. Coffin notes that he was buried in a Section H tomb. This suggests an underground chamber was constructed quite early. During a conservation project in the surrounding area, we unearthed what appeared to be a slate footstone for Dr. Coffin carefully buried just about where the tomb entrance is found. As noted above, a footstone marked the lower border of the grave and typically matched the headstone. It would usually be cut from the same source stone, the footstone being a miniature of the headstone and listing just the initials (sometimes

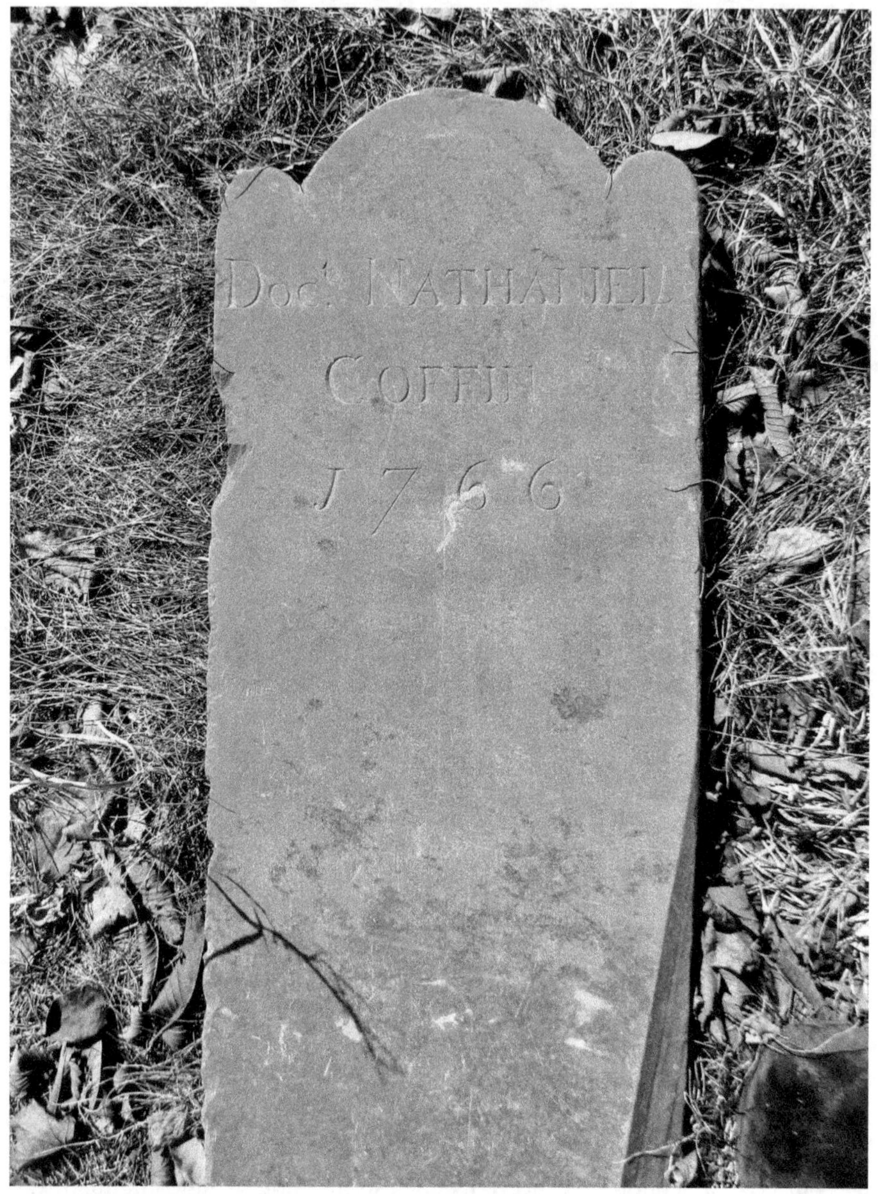

The 1766 marker for Dr. Nathaniel Coffin, discovered underground during conservation in 2016.

the name and date) of the deceased. Dr. Coffin's stone was inscribed as a typical footstone is, with only "Doc't. Nathaniel Coffin" and "1766" but no inscription or other details. We were thrilled to find this marker, which had likely not seen the light of day for well over two hundred years.

But why would Dr. Coffin need a footstone if he was buried in a tomb? The answer is that he wouldn't. This marker is curiously about double the length of a typical footstone, so it could have served another purpose. Was it the entrance marker for his underground tomb? Another possibility is that the tomb was constructed sometime after Dr. Coffin's 1766 death and that he had first been buried in the open ground with a headstone (now missing) and this footstone and then later moved into the tomb. If this is true, perhaps his original headstone is also buried in the same general area and will someday be unearthed.

Chapter 2

BOSTON MARKERS, BOSTON MAKERS

On Christmas Day 1821, mischievous fourteen-year-old Horatio Noyes visited Portland's First Parish Meeting House. He found the door to the tower unlocked and climbed the stairs to the open-air belfry. Then—according to witnesses on the street—he began to climb one of the pillars supporting the steeple. His adventure didn't last long; he lost his grip and fell seventy feet to the ground. He was "taken up speechless and apparently senseless" and brought to a nearby house but lived just an hour longer. Horatio was buried at Eastern Cemetery near his father, who'd passed a year earlier; the two are memorialized on a handsome slate grave marker decorated with an urn and willow found at plot D-60.

The area surrounding the landmark pine contains the oldest dated markers found at Eastern Cemetery. Nearby is a line of graves marked only with pieces of "found" stone (that is, fieldstone gathered by the family). Two pieces of found stone were crudely etched to create homemade markers. One is for Jonathan Wilson (possibly Madson), dated 1720, and another for three great-grandchildren of John Proctor, the first man hanged for witchcraft in Salem in 1692. The children on the Proctor stone—Sary, Thomas and Richard—died between 1741 and 1748, all under age ten. Their father, Benjamin, was born after the witch trials, but their grandfather Samuel was seven when his own father (John Proctor) was executed. Samuel was the first in this line to move to Portland. He died in 1765, but his grave location is not known.

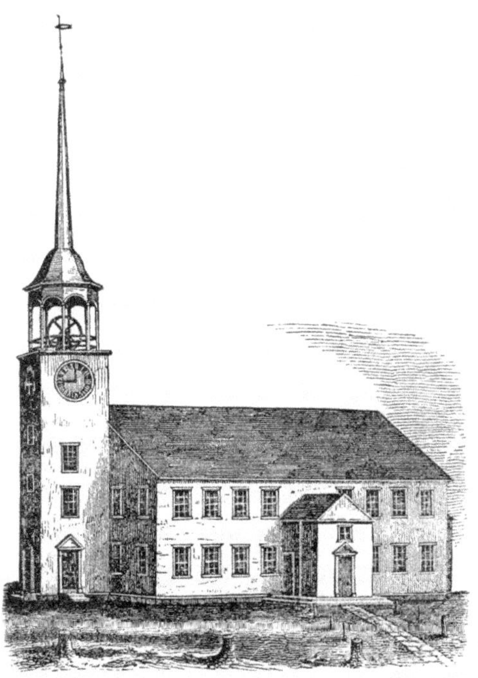

Left: Portland's First Parish Meeting House, site of Horatio Noyes's accidental death. *From the Portland City Guide.*

Below: The homemade grave marker for three Proctor children, who died in the 1740s. The stone has delaminated (split) and is badly eroded.

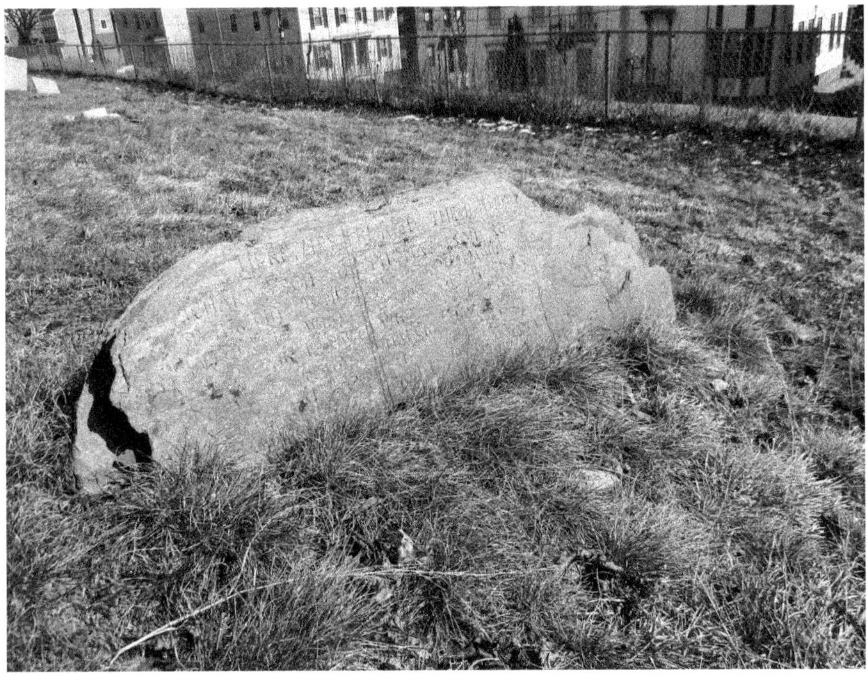

While we know burials occurred in the 1600s, burial records were not kept for well over a century, so researchers wishing to locate the oldest graves must rely on transcriptions from the few gravestones that have survived. The earliest surviving professionally carved gravestone is Mary Green's 1717 gray slate. Oddly, in 1940 the *Portland City Guide* noted, "A crumbling reddish-colored stone, its rim barely visible above the ground, marks the grave of Mrs. Mary Brown who died in 1718, the first recorded burial in the cemetery." I found no record of Mrs. Brown, yet if she was known as late as 1940, shouldn't her marker also have been recorded in Goodwin's 1890 survey? Further, Jordan has the first recorded burial as Nicholas Curwin from 1704. So Mrs. Brown, with her crumbling reddish-colored stone, is a mystery, but Mary Green is certainly not, and a visit to her 1717 grave is included on every tour.

There is a charming marker from 1718 for Stephen Larrabee. His design provided the inspiration for the Spirits Alive logo. Both his and Mary Green's stones came from carvers in Boston three hundred years ago and—thanks to the quality of the slate used—have survived beautifully. Both have early English spelling on their inscriptions ("ye" for "the"), and their carvers employed the use of ligatures (combining two letters into one).

No resident stonecutter was in Portland until 1800, so anyone who wanted a professionally carved marker would travel by sea to Boston to purchase it from one of the many stone stops there. While wealthier families had the means to make the trip, the vast majority of townspeople were poor and instead simply decorated graves with wood or found stone, if at all. People had plenty of other worries. Food supplies were unreliable, winters were severe and conflicts with natives persisted. Reverend Smith wrote in 1745 that the townspeople had "a constant expectation of the Indians doing mischief." Epidemics swept through the town, wiping out dozens at a time; Smith documented the outbreaks since he attended the sick and dying. His journal noted epidemics of throat distemper in the 1730s, smallpox in the 1750s, measles in the 1770s and whooping cough in the 1780s, among others.

We are fortunate to have about one hundred Boston-made grave markers from the 1700s in Eastern Cemetery. Jim Blachowicz, the preeminent researcher of Massachusetts stonecutters, has attributed about forty of those to fourteen Boston carvers, including Daniel Hastings, John Homer and John Lamson.

Boston stones are typically slate, with a "bedstead" shape (that is, shaped like a headboard), rounded shoulders, decorated borders and a winged skull or death's head design. The skulls and bones represent the mortal remains of

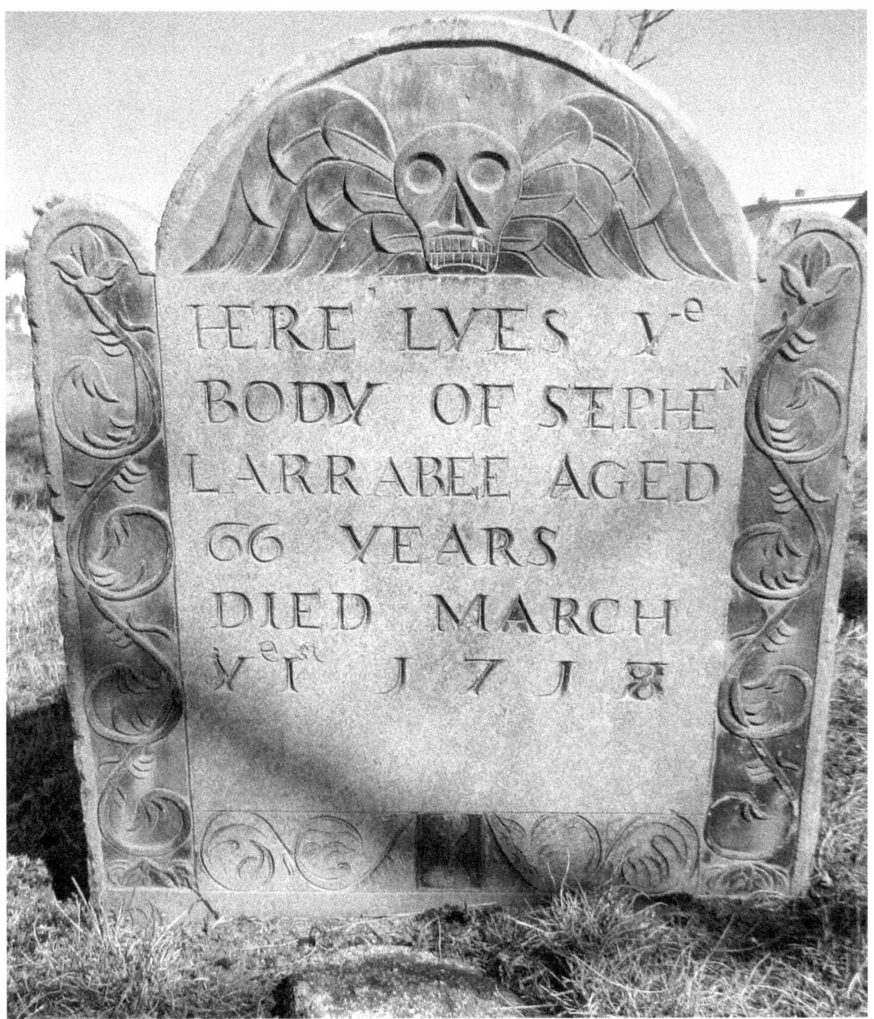

Stephen Larrabee's 1718 gravestone. Note the ligature in the word "Here" and the use of old English "lyes" and "ye."

the deceased, and the wings represent the flight of the soul to heaven. Stones for two of the Dow family's children who died in 1773 are extraordinary designs of skulls and crossed bones carved by Henry Christian Geyer of Boston. The design is frequently seen in the colonial graveyards of Boston, but we have just the two at Eastern Cemetery.

In the latter half of the century, carvers began to abandon the use of the icons that expressed the finality of death (skulls and bones) and shifted

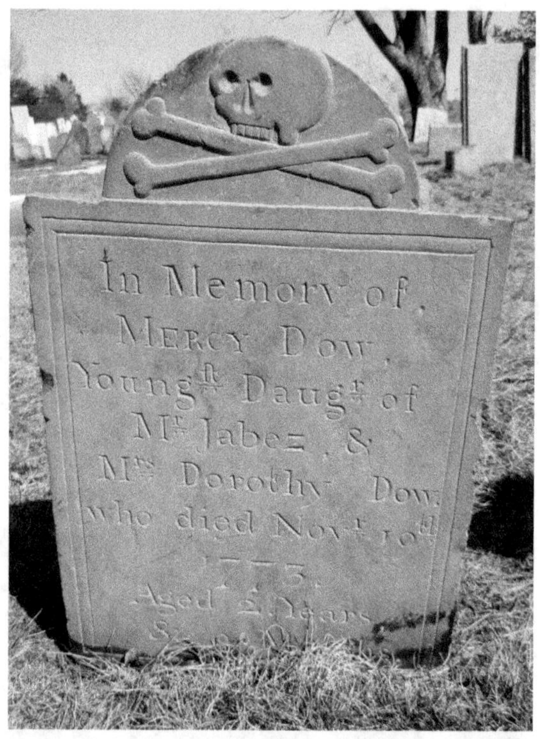

Right: A marker carved in Boston, circa 1773, for Mercy Dow featuring a skull and pair of bones, representing the finality of death. Her brother's marker is next to hers and has a similar design.

Below: The unusual "portrait stone" carved for Joseph Stockbridge, circa 1761, featuring a full figure with a bagwig to recognize his service in the court.

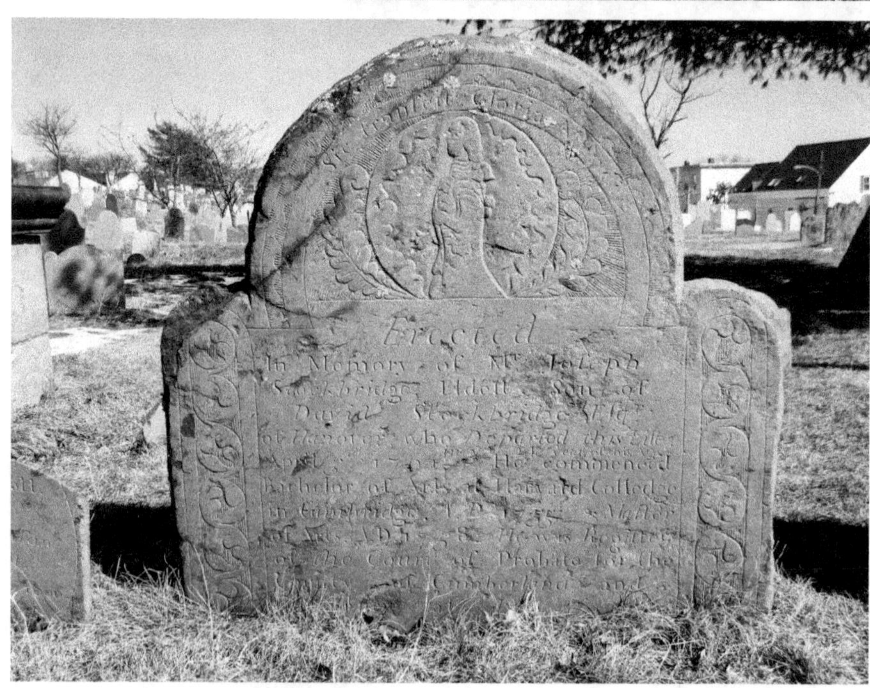

toward more spiritual images. Skulls were replaced with cherubic human faces or soul effigies that still bore wings to represent the soul's flight to heaven. Inscriptions tempered as well, so that "in memory of..." was used more frequently than "here lies mouldering in the dust..." and similar older phrases. Carvers also began to use full figures to represent the deceased, although these were not necessarily meant to be an actual likeness of the individual. Known as "portrait stones," they are quite rare. The best of the few at Eastern Cemetery is for Joseph Stockbridge, who graduated from Harvard in 1755 and served in Portland as the first register of probate. His massive red mudstone marker depicts him wearing a bagwig, signifying his work in the colonial court. He died very early in his career, at age twenty-four in 1761; Reverend Smith wrote that Stockbridge had experienced "a great sickness and mortality."

Another 1761 marker that is a one-of-a-kind in Portland memorializes Cornelius Bramhall. The soul effigy on his marker, carved by Asaph Soule, features large vacant eyes, no mouth and wild hair. Cornelius was the grandson of George Bramhall, the first settler of the west end of Portland who was killed in the 1689 conflict mentioned earlier. Cornelius's grandmother and her children (including Cornelius's father, Joshua,

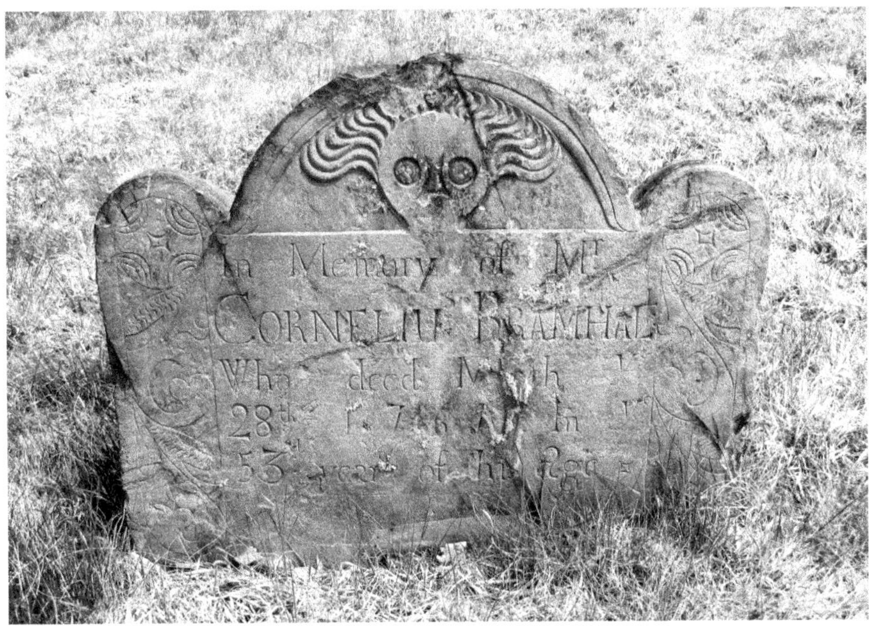

The marker carved for Cornelius Bramhall, circa 1761, by Asaph Soule. It's the only "soul effigy" of this type known in southern Maine.

who was just six at the time) escaped the attack and lived in Plymouth, Massachusetts. Both died there. I visited Plymouth and found the marker for Joshua at the Old Burial Ground. It is an exact match to Cornelius's stone. Joshua died in 1763, two years after Cornelius, and it's clear that the family ordered two stones from Asaph Soule around the same time, one of which stayed in Massachusetts, the other being shipped to Portland.

Boston-cut markers at Eastern Cemetery are limited to the eighteenth century; none are found for people who died in 1800 or after. This makes perfect sense, for stonecutter Bartlett Adams moved to Portland from Quincy, Massachusetts, in the fall of 1800.

Chapter 3

THE TOWN'S FIRST STONECUTTER

A "mad day of rejoicing" was underway in Portland on April 4, 1783. A notice had arrived from Boston stating that Congress was on the verge of ratifying a peace treaty with Great Britain. King George III was acknowledging the independence of the states, and the true conclusion of the Revolutionary War was in sight. The streets had erupted with revelers. Among them was forty-year-old Samuel Rollins, a mariner who was married with four children. Cannons fired incessantly throughout town—even within the residential sections—from morning until night. Samuel was standing near a cannon when it accidentally exploded; the debris from the blast broke his jaw and one of his arms. Unable to recover, he died four days later, on April 8. His grave marker has been lost.

Bartlett Adams's story is the subject of my first book. His shop was responsible for creating about a third of all the markers found today at Eastern Cemetery, so his work deserves review. Since the release of that book, I have gained confidence in identifying Bartlett's lettering in the 1820s and have attributed about 225 additional markers to him.

Bartlett was born in 1776 in Kingston, Massachusetts, and was trained in the art of stonecutting by his brother-in-law, also of that town. After his apprenticeship, he spent about five years as a journeyman in a shop in Quincy, Massachusetts, and he left behind about thirty-five grave markers that are found today in the cemeteries of Quincy and Milton.

In 1800, Bartlett came to Portland. He was twenty-four, single, skilled and intelligent. He was instantly very busy operating his own shop as

Portland's first resident stonecutter. While he supplied private homes with mantelpieces and hearths and furnished public buildings with keystones and other finished pieces, the gravestones he carved are plentiful and more easily found. My surveys of more than three hundred cemeteries in the region have resulted in an attributions list of about 1,800 gravestones carved in the Adams shop over a twenty-eight-year period.

At Eastern Cemetery, I've attributed just under seven hundred markers to Bartlett's shop. Of those, 10 percent are backdated, some to the 1770s—proof that Bartlett was satisfying the pent-up demand for gravestones that existed in Portland when he arrived. The ability of the townspeople to shop locally meant that the flow of finished gravestones from the Boston shops ended upon his arrival. And one by one, year by year, many of the crude grave markers of wood and found stone were replaced by his carvings.

Bartlett married Charlotte Neal in 1803, and seven children followed, but sadly, six predeceased them. Bartlett carved gravestones for the first three, and they're standing together in the cemetery. He died in 1828 at age fifty-one of unknown causes. He has a family tomb at the cemetery that was originally decorated with a table monument; today, its six columns are missing and only the sandstone and brick base remains.

Bartlett lived and worked on Portland Neck, but he also had a large farm in New Gloucester, about twenty-five miles due north. He spent almost two years there during the War of 1812 when business considerably slowed down. There he tended his orchard—a passion of his, I believe, given that he ran a side business selling fruit trees each spring at his shop in Portland.

BARTLETT ADAMS,

MAKES *Stone Stove Fire Places*—a medium between Franklin's and Pain's Patent Stoves—includes all the good qualities of both, without any of their inconveniences—ſaves one half the wood a common fire place conſumes, and be equally as warm and comfortable—and are a ſure remedy for ſmoaky rooms.

Portland, Dec. 31, 1803.

An advertisement placed by Bartlett Adams in 1803 for his stone stove fireplace, "a sure remedy for smoaky rooms."

STONE CUTTING,

EXECUTED IN ALL ITS BRANCHES, BY

BARTLETT ADAMS,

In Federal Street, near the corner of Court Street.

WHO, having replenished his stock, offers for sale,

6 elegant marble Chimney Pieces;
1 set marble Facings;
40 set of free-stone Hearths, Jambs & Mantels
50 pairs of ornamental and plain white marble Grave Stones;
35 pairs of dove marble Grave Stones;
3 white marble Tomb Tables;
1 white marble obelisk Monument;
75 pairs slate Grave Stones;
1800 soap stone Ink-stands;
2 Garden Rolls; 5 Paint Mills;—*ALSO*—
Paint Stones and Mullers; Door-sills; Window Caps and Sills; Steps; Spout Stones; Grindstones; Scotch Hone, and other stones for Currier's use.

N. B. Orders from any part of the State, for any Stone Work in his line, executed at the shortest notice and on reasonable terms.

Aug. 6, 1822 3w

An advertisement placed by Bartlett Adams in 1822 soon after restocking his shop.

Two of Bartlett's nephews, one of his brothers and a handful of other carvers and apprentices worked with Bartlett cutting gravestones over the twenty-eight years he owned the shop. I've been able to isolate the style of many of these men and am now able to identify gravestones by their carvers. It's an evolving effort with sometimes inexact results, but the more we study the markers, the better we understand who created them.

Piecing together the story of someone who lived two hundred years ago is an interesting challenge. Fortunately, Bartlett frequently advertised his business in the newspaper. He also placed notices when he left the shop in the hands of his nephews, when he cautioned people from doing business with one of his apprentices whom he had dismissed from service and even when he needed help finding a cow that had wandered off his property. While my first book was being printed, Art Gaffar of the Maine Charitable Mechanic Association found two ads that I had never seen. One describes an innovative new kitchen stove, and the other—which was placed after his shop had been restocked—shows the variety of products Bartlett offered customers.

I've done dozens of Bartlett Adams lectures and cemetery walks since 2014. While he was a man who once was unknown to most, the talks, walks and publication of the book all put a spotlight on him. He is certainly better known today. He was underappreciated in his time, serving a utilitarian role of supplying people with gravestones. Now we know that he was a talented artist of a craft that has nearly died (pun intended). What a thrill when someone shows up for a tour of the cemetery and asks, "Isn't this where Bartlett Adams gravestones are found?"

Chapter 4

THE BURYING GROUND

After 1795

Twice in 1848, people simply fell dead in the street. Samuel Whittier was first, on April 13. His cause of death at age sixty-four was "apoplexy" (a stroke). Oliver Blake followed on June 17. He was a painter who was in his mid-fifties when he "fell dead in the street in a fit." Whittier's grave is now unmarked; Blake's grave at plot D-23 has an eroded marble headstone.

Just five years before Bartlett Adams moved to town, the cemetery was substantially expanded. Reverend Thomas Smith, Portland's first minister, owned the land between the Burying Ground and Back (now Congress) Street. It was three-plus acres of fairly level field. Smith allowed a path to be run across his land from the street to the cemetery so people wishing to visit the burial ground could access it either from the traditional southern border or through his field to the north. The path was named "Funeral Lane" and still exists today as the main pathway for visitors who enter through the front gate. Reverend Smith was asked to convey the property to the town for use as a burial ground and did so on his deathbed in 1795. It would be a more interesting story if Reverend Smith was the first to be buried in the newly acquired burial land that was once his own, but instead he was buried near the other settlers by the landmark pine. The box tomb monument that rests on his plot holds a newer ledger slab; the original had broken by 1860 and has been replaced at least once.

With the acquisition of the reverend's land (Sections A and B on the visitors' map), the town's available burial space more than doubled, providing

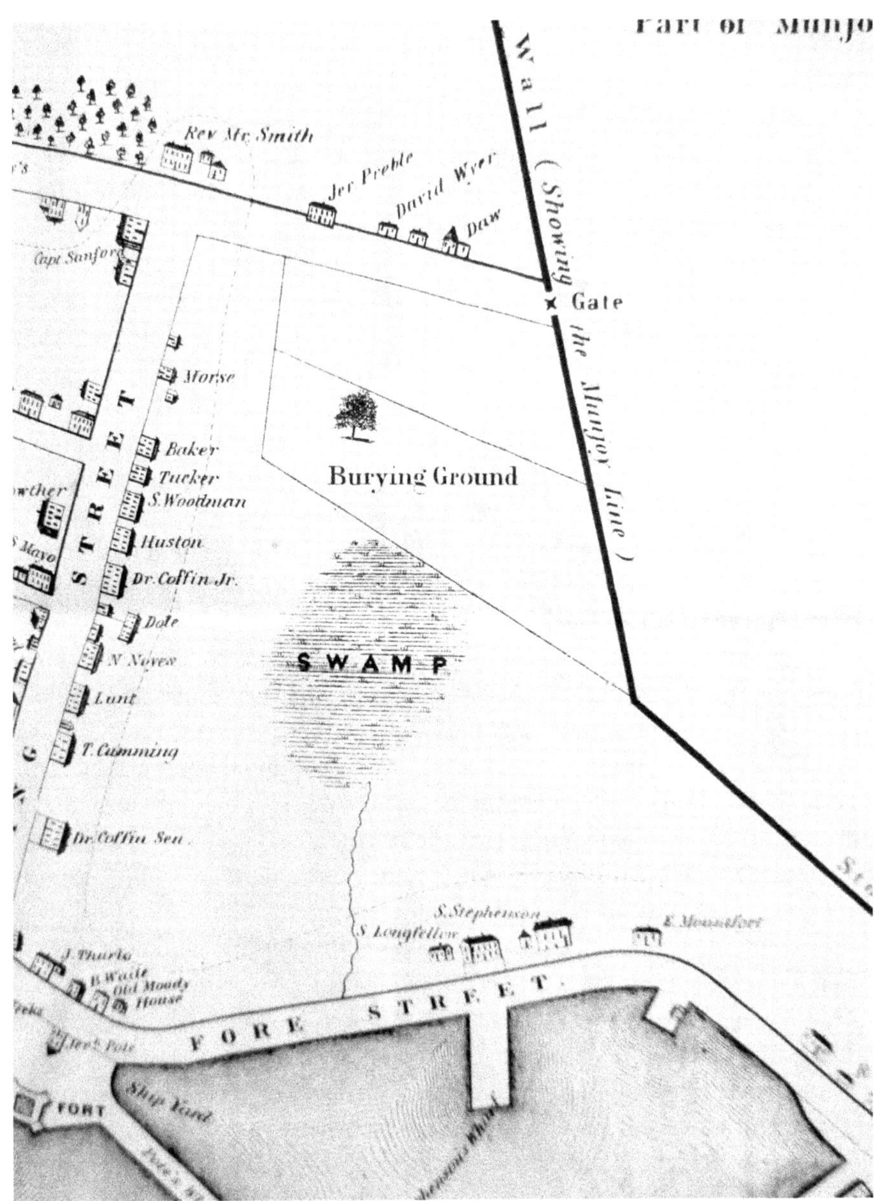

Map detail showing the town's Burying Ground in 1775. Reverend Smith's land was just above it and became part of the cemetery in 1795. *From* The History of Portland *by William Willis. Courtesy of Bill Dalbec.*

much relief to those worried about finding room to put their loved ones. The Burying Ground then encompassed almost seven acres. Today, we refer to Sections A and B as the "new section" (keeping in mind that "new" is 1795—a fact that helps visitors on tours gain perspective about how old the burial ground really is), and we call Sections C through L the "old section." I use those terms for the remainder of the book.

Section B was put to use right away for burials, except for a patch of land on its western edge, where a tool house stood, and another patch just inside the Congress Street gate. The tool house did not last, but the patch near the gate stayed free of graves and would—fifty years later—serve as the site of the city's first receiving tomb. The large, level expanse of Section A was initially maintained as a public common, where military training exercises occurred, children played and livestock grazed. A town pound was fenced off there to hold stray animals; even the town's pillory and whipping post were located there. By about 1825, the field had begun to be converted for burials, and as Goold wrote, "the living gave up their playground to the dead."

The expansion brought about a few key changes to the cemetery. First among them was obviously the extra space, another was an effort to better maintain records and a third was the introduction of narrow pathways (in the old section) running up the slope from the original southern border. The pathway Smith had allowed to be cut through his field ran straight in from the street, originally ending at the northern edge of the old section. But in the city's possession, Funeral Lane was extended in an easterly direction. Today, visitors still walk straight in from the Congress Street gate on the original path to the edge of the old section, but the lane now takes a sharp left and runs all the way to the back gate on Mountfort Street.

The town selectmen also authorized a plan to lay out the burial ground into regular rows and divisions; the old section had had no such plan, leaving graves scattered in irregular rows. Jordan wrote that the selectmen ended the practice of reserved family lots. In order to maximize space, they ordered that people be buried one next to another as they died, regardless of family affiliation. That must not have settled well with the townspeople, and it does not appear to have been enforced. At least thirty-two family lots are found in Sections A and B, each consisting of four to eight graves. Many of these were set off with fencing, some of which remains today.

The Field of Family Tombs

Another solution for families seeking to keep loved ones together came with the acquisition of Reverend Smith's land: the development of the series of underground family tombs in Section A. Over a thirty-year period, eighty-six tombs organized in four rows were constructed underground along the border between the old and new sections of the cemetery. Each tomb is approximately twelve feet long, six feet wide and six feet tall and has a private entrance that is accessed by removing the sod and wooden planks over the stairway and then descending into the chamber.

Each tomb was designed to hold up to thirty bodies; at capacity, the coffins would have been packed in like sardines. Though today we are not allowed to enter these tombs, one was opened in 2010 following a cave-in. While the investigators were inside inspecting the structure, they noted the presence of human remains for two individuals. Details and photographs are found in the Master Plan and make for a fascinating read, but equally

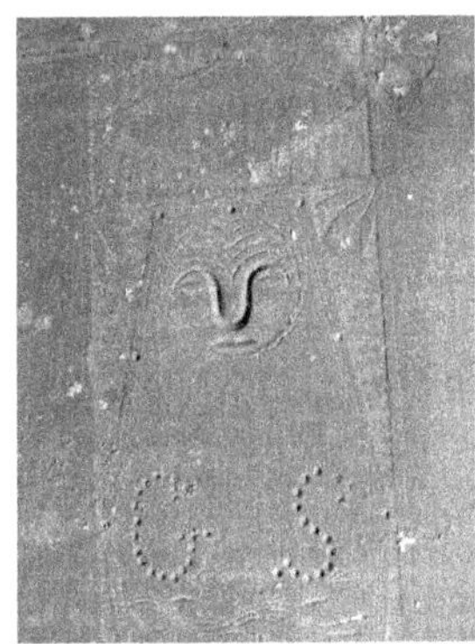

Above: Detail of an 1814 marker for George Smith found in Vermont, carved to feature a coffin with a round viewing glass.

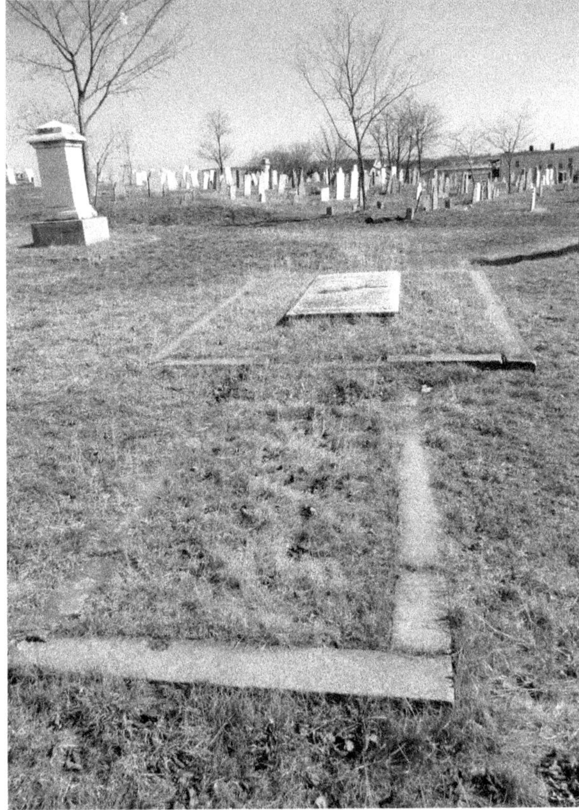

Right: An underground tomb in Section A. Note the border stones provide an exact outline of the chamber, with the smaller portion in the foreground framing the tomb's private stairway and the larger portion in the background framing the tomb itself.

interesting was the discovery of a glass viewing plate. With embalming not in widespread use until the Civil War, people needed to be buried quickly after death because of the rapid deterioration of the body. One way to delay the burial so that family members could extend the period of mourning was to cut a hole in the wooden coffin near the deceased's face and insert a piece of glass. This allowed mourners to see the deceased in the sealed coffin without the worry of the odor of decaying flesh. I found a wonderful grave marker in an early Vermont graveyard that features the image of a typical six-sided coffin with a viewing glass. The face of the deceased is easily seen.

Families decorated their tombs as they wished. A variety of monuments are found, including obelisks, pedestals, table tombs (none of which still have their columns), ledgers and box tombs (see Appendix A). Though box tombs appear to be aboveground burial containers, they are simply decorative monuments. No bodies at Eastern Cemetery are entombed above ground level.

THE SEXTON'S JOURNAL

Cemetery sexton William Hoadley served as superintendent of Eastern Cemetery from 1897 until his death in 1912. Over his fifteen years in that role, he entered most (perhaps all) of the underground tombs. In addition, when people visited the grave sites of their loved ones, he often inquired about their family histories. He left behind a lengthy journal, now in the collections at Maine Historical Society. It contains the listings of tombs' occupants, based primarily on Hoadley's transcriptions of the inscribed metal coffin plates he found during his underground visits. It also contains family histories. For the cemetery enthusiast, genealogist or fan of Eastern Cemetery, paging through the journal can easily take up an afternoon's time, and it is well worth seeing.

The field of family tombs at Eastern Cemetery is quite special. I've never seen an arrangement quite like it in any other New England colonial graveyard, although something similar to this design may exist. We always show the field of tombs to our visitors on tours.

Overcrowding

The pressure on the town to have adequate burial space was addressed through expansion, construction of the high-capacity tombs and innovative ideas such as burying some people two to a grave. Still, as soon as new ground was added, it would be filled, and eventually it became clear that a second cemetery was necessary on the Neck. In 1829, the town purchased the land that held the Vaughan family's burial lot on Bramhall Hill—on the west end of town—and began to develop it as the second cemetery on the peninsula. It was around this time that we began to see use of the name "Eastern Cemetery," in place of Burying Ground, and "Western Cemetery" to differentiate the two.

Eastern Cemetery stayed active into the mid-1800s, when the city decided to close it to new burials. Except for remaining spaces in family lots or tombs, all plots were filled. An article in the *Portland Transcript* reported, "The Eastern Cemetery is so crowded with the dead that the Superintendent of Burials wishes to appropriate to the use of residents, the lots now taken up

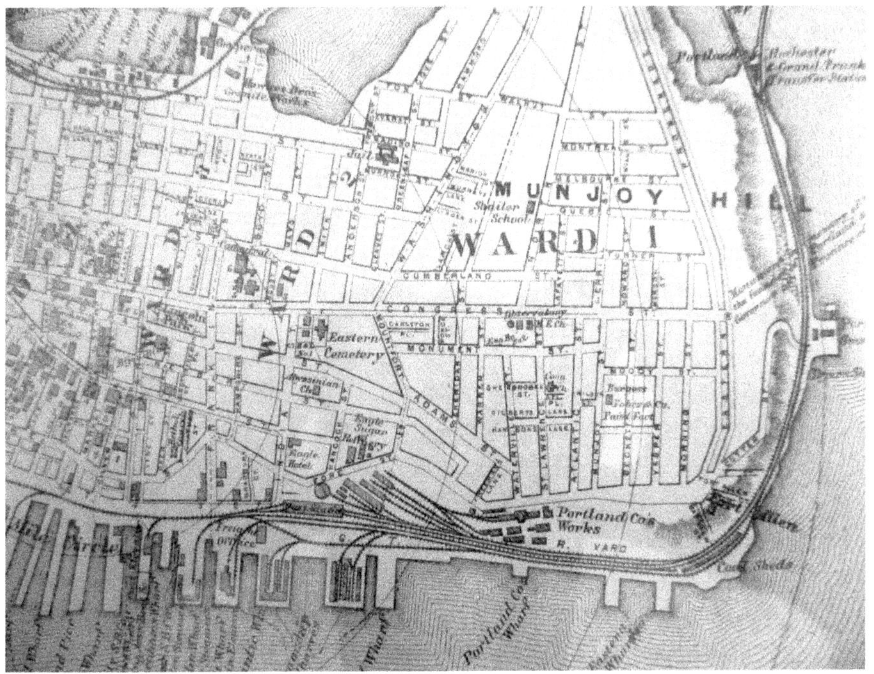

Portland map, circa 1890, of the eastern end of Portland Neck. Eastern Cemetery is dead center of this image. *Courtesy of Bill Dalbec.*

by non-residents. We believe some portions of this burial ground have been dug over two or three times. A new cemetery on Munjoy, or beyond Tukey's Bridge, seems needed for the use of residents in the eastern part of the city." Fortunately, Western Cemetery had opened, and its twelve acres became the new primary burial ground on the peninsula.

Loss of Land

The final change in the landscape of the burial ground came after the Great Fire of 1866, when all the structures on the southern border of the cemetery were burned to the ground. Recall that the southern border had been the primary access to the cemetery from its inception until the new ground was purchased in 1795 from Reverend Smith. But the southern access points were completely cut off to pedestrians during the reconstruction that followed the fire. Instead of rebuilding homes, the city decided to clear the land and extend Federal Street from downtown to Munjoy Hill. In the process, some of the original hillside of the old Burying Ground was carved away, and the overall size of the cemetery was reduced somewhat, to today's six acres.

There is debate among historians regarding the removal of human remains during this construction project. Some state with certainty that remains were taken, while the Master Plan says there was "no wholesale removal of remains." Given the large amount of land involved, I do believe that *some* decomposed remains of early settlers were taken away when the hillside was removed and replaced by the massive stone retaining wall that exists today.

Five burial records include references to grave sites near where Hancock Street intersected with the cemetery. In fact, the 1847 record for Hannah Parsons reads, "Buried south of alley to Hancock Street." Mention of an alley means that we can place one of the pre-fire pathway entrances into the cemetery at the intersection of Hancock and Federal Streets. Hancock Street is across from the cemetery at about the midpoint of its southern border. Standing street level at the intersection today, it becomes clear that a great amount of earth was removed during the post-fire reconstruction, as the retaining wall is very tall at that point.

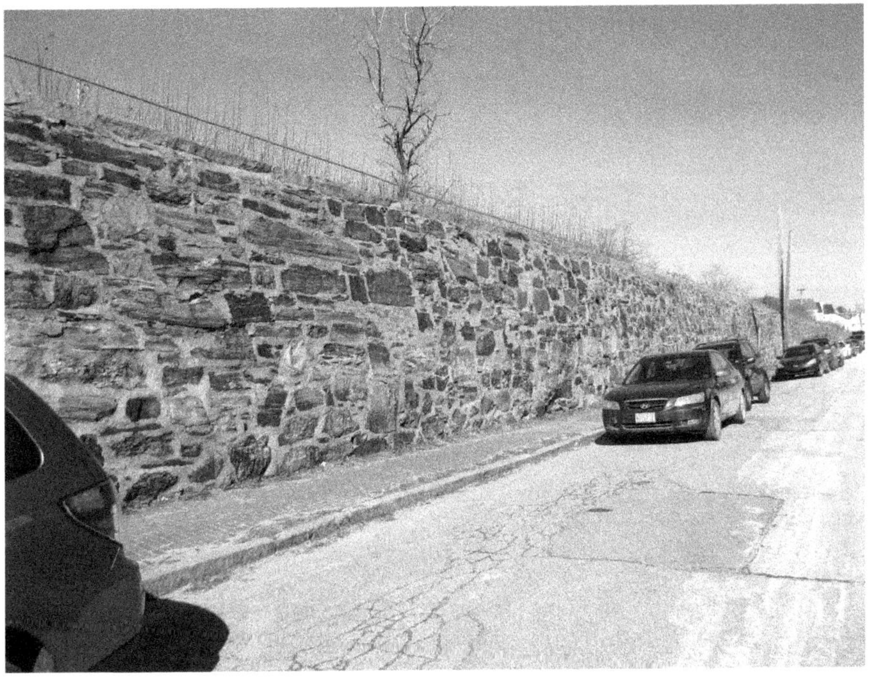

A current view of the stone retaining wall on Federal Street near the Hancock Street intersection. It was erected following the Great Fire of 1866 and required the removal of some of the ancient burial ground.

The Last Burial

With Western Cemetery and then Evergreen, Forest City and others coming into existence in the 1800s, the pressure was truly off Eastern Cemetery, and burials significantly declined in the last half of the century. The height of use had been in the 1820s, with seven hundred recorded burials. In each following decade, the number reduced, and by the 1870s, just over one hundred burials occurred. Six burials occurred between 1890 and 1899, and only twenty-two burials were recorded after the turn of the century; the final known was Henry Blake, placed in his family's tomb in 1962.

CHAPTER 5

THE DEAD HOUSE AND RECEIVING TOMB

Nicholas Everett, a native of Pennsylvania, was already a widower by his mid-thirties. He moved to Portland to work on the railroad and in 1850 was living at Alexander Gray's Atlantic Boarding House in Portland, along with eleven other single adults. The 1858 Portland directory listed his occupation as road master for the railroad. On January 14, 1860, he was killed in a railroad accident. Since the ground was frozen at Eastern Cemetery, his body was stored in the city tomb until spring thaw. Then, he was moved to his final resting place, plot A-21-9.

Maine winters are typically harsh; the ground can be frozen from Thanksgiving through April, limiting the season for digging graves to about eight months. I once read that some colonial communities pre-dug many graves each fall for any townspeople who might die during the winter. This allowed for temporary placement of bodies—covered with snow—until spring thaw, when they'd be moved to their final locations. What was the practice in Portland? No answers are found in the sources researched for this book, but I suspect that some families stored loved ones in their own barns. I also think that a storage shed was probably located within the cemetery itself. A likely spot for one is at the present-day site of the Dead House and Receiving Tomb. While the area surrounding that site was used for burials, the site itself remained free of interments.

Regardless of how bodies had been stored in the past, a permanent solution was found in 1849 with the construction of the city's Receiving Tomb. It was built just inside and to the right of the Congress Street gate.

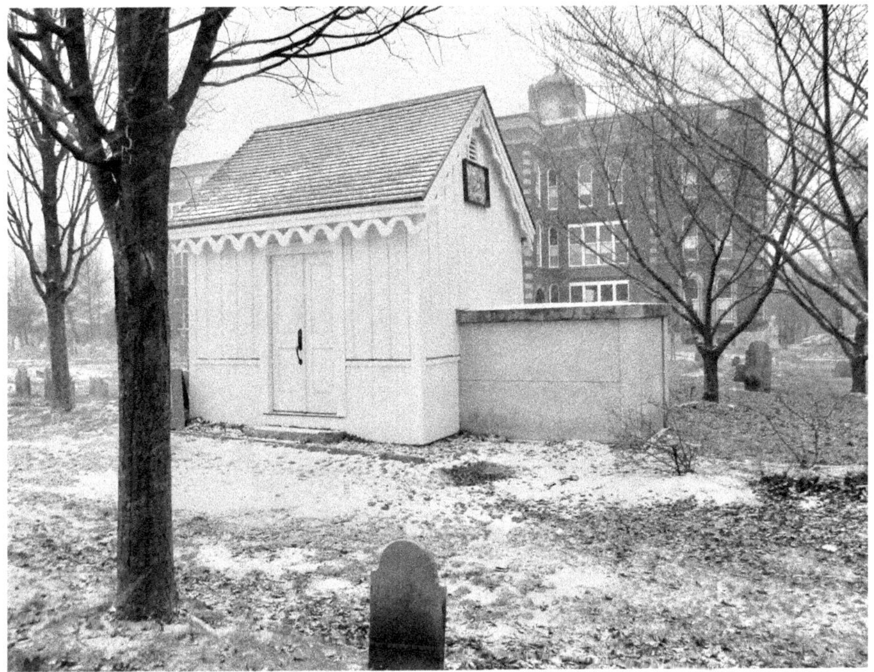

A current view of the Dead House and the aboveground granite portion of the Receiving Tomb.

The aboveground portion of the structure consists of massive granite slabs that protect the stairway down into the chamber. The presence of pins embedded into the stone at the entrance tells us that there was a set of double doors that opened outward. A set of long hooks on the inside walls tells us that there was a second set of double doors that laid flush to the ground in order to completely seal the chamber.

The tomb is constructed of fieldstone and brick with an arched ceiling. At twenty-one feet long, eleven feet wide and seven feet tall, it could accommodate eighty coffins over the winter. While we are unable to bring visitors into the tomb during tours, we do use the space for storage of "orphan stones." Sometimes while doing conservation, we will unearth a broken piece of a gravestone, a stray footstone or even a complete marker. We do our best to find out where these pieces belong, and when possible, we return them to their original locations. But some have no identifiable markings on them and we just don't know where they go. If it is safe to leave the piece where we found it (meaning unlikely to get hit by a mower or cause a tripping hazard for wanderers), we may do so. Otherwise, it goes into the

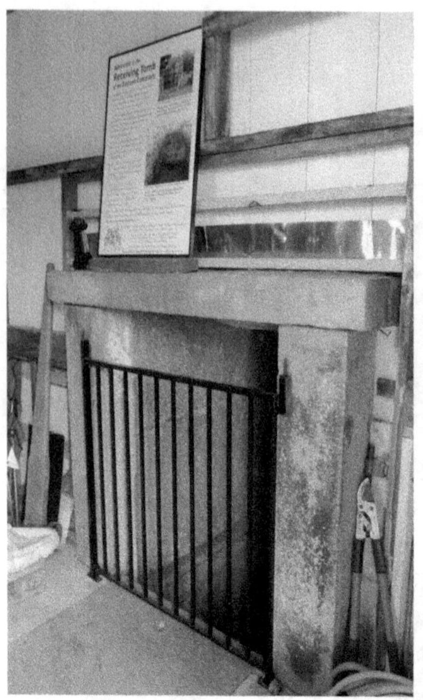

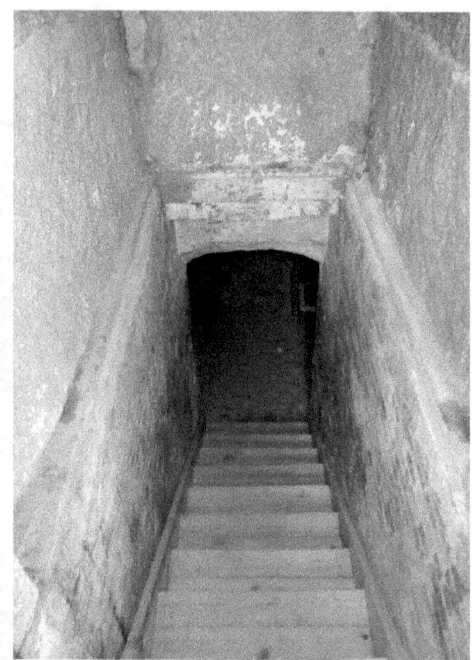

Left: The entrance to the Receiving Tomb as seen from inside the Dead House. *Courtesy of Janet Alexander.*

Right: The stairway down into the tomb.

Receiving Tomb for temporary storage. One day we hope to install shelving in the tomb so that we can better catalogue and store the orphans.

The giant granite box that protects the tomb stairway stood alone on the site for about twenty years. Around 1870, the city constructed a storage shed at the tomb entrance. Known as the "Dead House," this shed serves a double purpose. Not only does it shelter the entrance to the tomb, but it also provides useable space for storage of gardening tools and conservation supplies. Today, it makes an ideal meeting point for visitors taking a guided tour.

The Dead House got a much-needed upgrade in 2015 and 2016. The building was completely dismantled, a concrete floor was poured, the roof was replaced and a new wrought-iron gate was placed. Earlier, the city installed a water line just outside the front door of the house. Conservation work requires lots of water, and until this water line was installed, Spirits Alive volunteers hauled in buckets of water by hand.

The Receiving Tomb was used for about forty years. In 1868, the city charged undertakers four dollars to store a body over the winter. Jordan

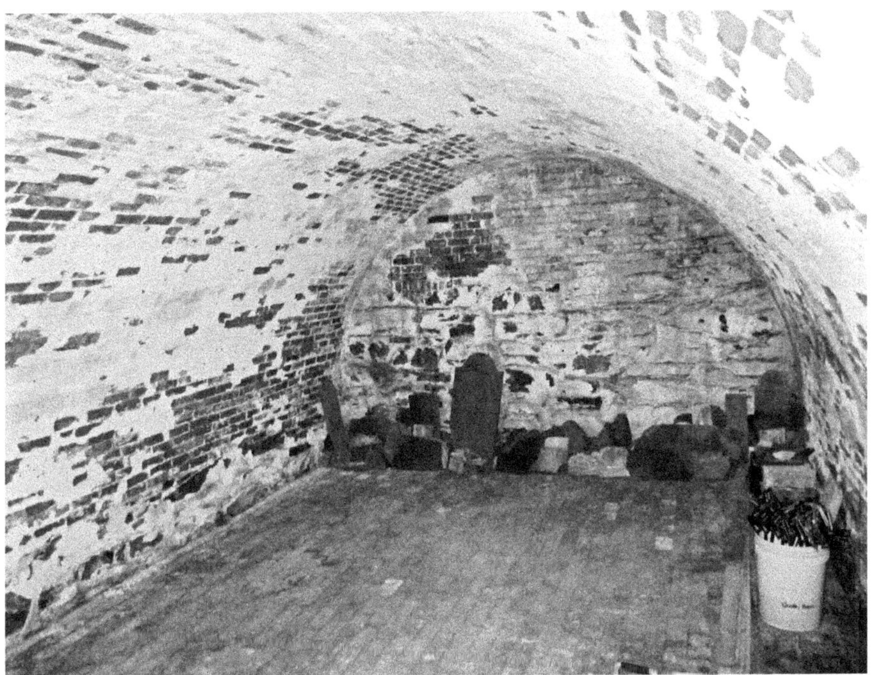

The interior of the Receiving Tomb, constructed in 1849 to house up to eighty bodies over the winter. Note the orphan stones along the back wall.

wrote that the first corpse brought into the tomb was that of Albert G. Smith, a twenty-seven-year-old man who died on September 7, 1849. It wasn't winter yet, so it's likely Mr. Smith's stay lasted just a day or two while his permanent grave was being dug. No further records are found for him, so we don't know if he ended up at Eastern, Western or Evergreen Cemetery.

Problems with record-keeping for Portland burials persisted into the late 1800s. Jordan's *Burial Records of Eastern Cemetery...* includes a roster of nearly one thousand people whose remains were temporarily placed in the Receiving Tomb over its forty-year use but whose final resting places were not recorded by the city.

Chapter 6

FIVE MEN HANGED FOR MURDER

Details about Jane Read are scarce, but we know her life was short. She died at age five on February 21, 1849, while living with two dozen other girls at the Female Orphan Asylum in Portland. Her death was caused by "dropsy in the head" (an abnormal accumulation of fluid). Without a family to provide a gravestone at Eastern Cemetery, she was buried the following spring in an unmarked grave.

Thomas Bird is generally recognized as being the first man hanged under the authority of the United States Constitution. He was executed in Portland in 1790 for murdering his master, the captain of a slave trade ship. But Bird was neither the first nor the last to be hanged for murder; four other men buried in unmarked graves at Eastern Cemetery met the same fate.

Solomon Goodwin (1723–1772)

The first was Solomon Goodwin, born in 1723 in Berwick, Maine, a riverside town on the border of New Hampshire, about forty miles southwest of Portland. He married Abigail Hooper there in 1747; she was five years younger than he. The couple had at least four children, three boys and a girl, over about twenty years. Though details about Solomon Goodwin are scarce, his name does appear in a half dozen court cases in the 1750s, involving claims of trespass and debts owed.

Perhaps those legal troubles are what brought about a move for the Goodwin family. At the time of his crime, Solomon was living northeast of Portland in the town of Bowdoinham, where he was a trapper. On May 25, 1772, he was on a trapping expedition, canoeing up the Kennebec River with David Wilson and another man. Goodwin and Wilson had a disagreement of some sort, which escalated into an argument. Solomon lost his temper and swung his oar, striking Wilson on the left temple and eye. According to the court records, Wilson received a "mortal wound three inches in length, two inches in width and one inch in depth." The force of the blow threw him into the river, where he drowned. Their companion reported the incident to the local authorities once ashore, stating that Solomon had done nothing to try to rescue Wilson from the water.

Solomon Goodwin initially escaped jail but was apprehended and tried. He was convicted of capital murder and sentenced to hang in July, but with a great many people believing he'd been wrongfully convicted, his death sentence was reprieved three times. Reverend Samuel Deane's journal includes these notes: "August 2. I prepared and preached a

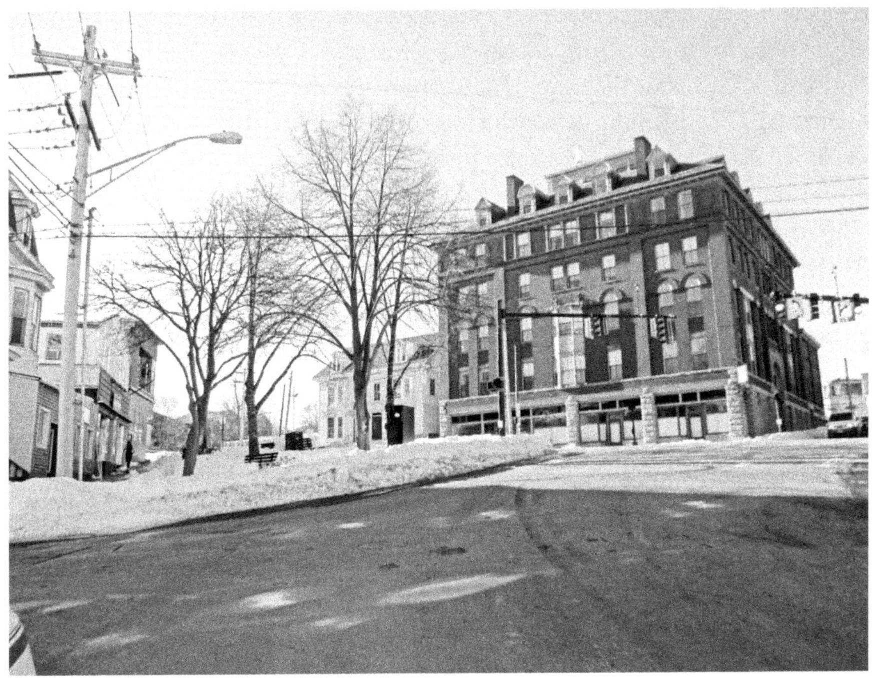

A view of Haggett's Hill, site of Portland's first gallows, now a busy intersection in a heavily developed area of town.

sermon for Goodwin, but he did not come"; "August 8. The prisoner came to the meeting"; and "August 10. Guard kept at the goal [jail] on account of the mob."

A gallows was constructed on Haggett's Hill (now near where Deering Avenue intersects Congress Street in the west end of the city). A sermon immediately before the execution cautioned the crowd against "intemperate drinking, quarreling, and keeping wicked company." Solomon Goodwin's final words were, "I had no intention to kill Wilson with the blow that unhappily proved to be his death." Goodwin's execution on November 12, 1772, was documented in Deane's journal as having been attended by "many people, several thousands." The newspaper reported the crowd at six thousand, the largest-ever gathering in town.

Thomas Bird (1749–1790)

Thomas Bird was next in line. His story is fully told by Jerry Genesio in his 2010 book, *Portland Neck: The Hanging of Thomas Bird.* Genesio's account comes from his study of the handwritten records of the incident found at the National Archives in Waltham, Massachusetts.

Bird, an Englishman, was a lifelong mariner who had served on many ships, embarking from both English and American ports. During the Revolutionary War, he was captured, impressed into service and released—more than once. His most fateful journey began in 1787, when he joined the crew of a slave trader bound for Africa. The *Mary* was under the command of Captain John Connor, who had brought on Bird and five other seamen for the journey.

The crossing to Africa took nine weeks. Once there, Connor sailed up rivers in search of slaves, gold and ivory. On one of these excursions, three of Bird's crew mates became ill and were sent ashore. With half of his crew incapacitated, Captain Connor decided to anchor offshore. Over the course of the ensuing four months, Connor spent much of his own time ashore; one night, he returned to find none of the crew on watch. He became enraged, beating one of Bird's crew mates to near death and leaving him on the deck. The next day, his refusal to allow the failing crewman any water resulted in the injured seaman's death. Captain Connor ordered the others to throw the man's body overboard, but when Bird and his companion refused, the captain beat the companion and threatened Bird with the same. Eventually, the *Mary* was restored to full complement and set sail, but Bird reported being the recipient of the captain's ongoing cruelty, leading to his attempt to escape. He was captured and returned to the *Mary*—no doubt punished further still—which continued its journey along the African coastline.

Bird's account of his life aboard the ship includes frequent verbal and physical abuse by the captain, including one specific threat that Connor would kill him if he failed to properly maneuver the ship. Bird was not up to the particular task, and when he told the captain he needed help from his mates, the captain refused him. That must have been the last straw, for that night Captain Connor was shot while sleeping in his cot. His body was thrown overboard off the African coast.

So how is it that an English sailor at sea off Africa came to be hanged in Portland? Once the captain was out of the picture, another crewman took command of the *Mary* and decided to sail across the Atlantic to resource-rich Brazil. He died en route, so the others took control and sailed westward toward North America. They reached landfall in Maine in the summer of 1789 and anchored offshore at a few points, as close to Portland as Willard Beach in South Portland.

It became clear to the local naval officer and collector of customs that something was amiss when he approached the *Mary* but the ship took to the sea to avoid him. Two vessels then set out to capture the *Mary* and successfully brought it back to port. The four aboard—Bird and two other seamen, plus a young African boy—were taken into custody. Bird was charged with piracy and murder, another charged with aiding him. The two spent months in jail. Bird told the judge, "Hanson, Huddy and myself killed him at night. The Captain was killed by musket balls fired out of one gun that the Captain had loaded that afternoon. There were three guns in all fired at him. I then about twelve or one at night assisted in throwing him over. William Huddy, Hanson, and myself did it."

Only Bird was found guilty; his companion was released. The judge's lengthy statement ended with, "The Sentence which the law has affixed to your crime, and which this Court now awards against you is this: That you go from hence to the prison whence you came, and from thence to the place of Execution on Friday, the twenty-fifth day of June instant; and there be hanged by the neck until you are dead."

Bird's lawyers attempted to have the sentence reversed, given that this was the first such conviction after the establishment of the U.S. Constitution. Bird appealed to President George Washington, writing, "Yesterday I was tried and found guilty of the crime that the District Judge, a few hours since,

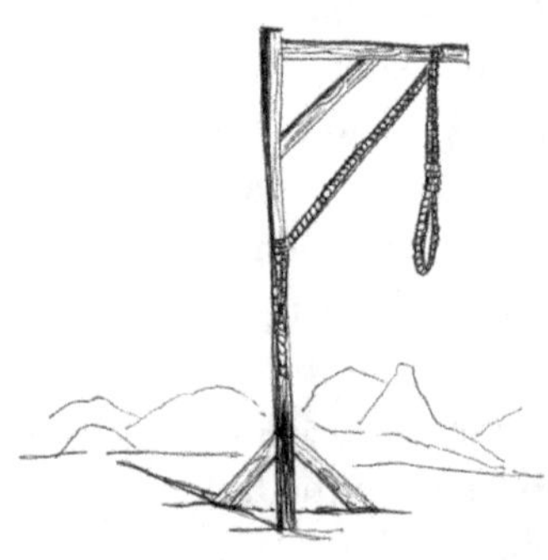

A typical gallows of the eighteenth century. *Sketch by Holly Doggett.*

pronounced the fatal sentence that still rings in my ears and harrows up my soul, the sentence of death." But Washington found no reason to issue a pardon or suspend the time of execution.

While awaiting his end, Bird was said to have occupied some of his time carving wooden toys for the sons of the jailhouse keeper. On the morning of his execution, Thomas Bird was interviewed by the editor of the Portland newspaper. Though he admitted having lived "an irreligious, wicked life, profaning the name of God, lying and drinking to excess," he changed his story about the fateful night aboard the *Mary*, claiming that he'd slept through Captain Connor's final night alive and that he knew nothing of his death.

Thomas Bird was hanged on June 25, 1790, from the same gallows that had been used for Goodwin. His execution was witnessed by three to four thousand people. His body was buried in an unmarked grave in the town's Burying Ground, today's Eastern Cemetery.

Joseph Drew (1783–1808)

Third in line was blacksmith Joseph Drew. Unlike Goodwin and Bird before him, Joseph Drew is not listed in Jordan's *Burial Records*. But he was hanged just steps from Eastern Cemetery in 1808 for the murder of Deputy Sheriff Ebenezer Parker of Cape Elizabeth. And since there was only one cemetery on Portland's peninsula, his remains surely were interred there.

Parker was on duty in January 1808, tracking down a man named Levi Quinby (sometimes Quimby) for debts he owed. Quinby was hiding out in Drew's blacksmith shop in Saccarappa (now Westbrook), and when Parker entered the shop to deliver a warrant, Drew tried to protect his friend by attacking Parker. He struck Parker on the head with a forge hammer. As Parker stumbled forward, Drew delivered a second blow to the head. Parker fell but did not die in the shop. He languished for a week before passing at the age of forty-eight, the first deputy to lose his life in the line of duty in Portland.

Joseph Drew's trial was held in May 1808 in the meetinghouse of the Second Parish, and after a long trial, he was convicted and sentenced to hang. A gallows was constructed on Munjoy Hill, nearer to the cemetery than the one that had been used for Goodwin and Bird. Joseph Drew was the first and only man to lose his life on the Munjoy Hill gallows. On July 20, 1808, the day before he was executed, he made a confession to be published in the newspaper. He said, "I fervently pray, if so great a sinner may look up to God, that these bitter regrets, and this glimmering hope, may be some consolation to my parents, and especially to my poor mother, if she yet survives the event of my condemnation; and that the sight of these [written] lines, when I am no more, may restrain their other children from the errors and vices which suffered not their ill-fated brother to 'live out half his days' and stamped infamy upon his memory." He admitted to living a life of corrupt and irascible passions fueled by temper yet wrote that through his time in jail he had been visited by many ministers who had taught him repentance.

He said, "My liberty is restrained in this gloomy cell! My hands in irons!... Tomorrow is the day of my death. At one o'clock, I shall be led from this prison to the place of execution; and at three o'clock shall be launched into eternity!"

The newspaper reported that at one o'clock on his final day, he emerged from prison dressed in a white robe and cap and became greatly agitated at the sight of his coffin and the great crowd that had gathered. He burst into tears and cried out, "Life is Sweet! Life is Sweet!" He walked the half mile from jail to the gallows accompanied by the county sheriff and

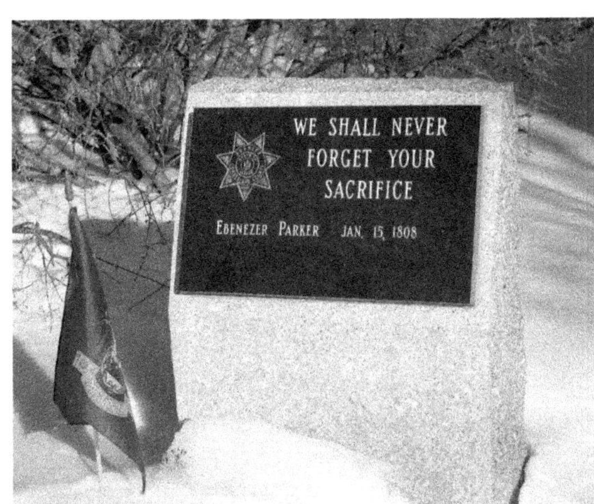

The commemorative marker for Deputy Sheriff Ebenezer Parker, first to die in the line of duty. It's located at the front door of the county sheriff's office in Portland.

many of his officers, ministers, the wooden cart carrying his coffin and the masses of spectators. When he arrived at the gallows, he climbed the ladder and awaited the sheriff's reading of his death warrant. When asked if he had anything to say, Joseph Drew made no reply, but "his lips were seen under the margin of his cap continually moving in prayer to the very last moment." A few minutes before three o'clock, the plank on which he stood was let go and "dropped him into eternity." The great crowd was said to have been completely silent at the end, the scene being "awful and impressive beyond description, as most who were present had never seen anything of the kind before."

Two hundred years after his murder, Ebenezer Parker was honored by the Cumberland County Sheriff's Office with a monument recognizing his service and ultimate sacrifice.

ABRAHAM COX (CIRCA 1790–1858) AND PETER WILLIAMS (1830–1858)

Fifty years after Joseph Drew paid for his crime with his life, two more met the same fate: Abraham Cox, a black man born a slave on St. Martin's Island around 1790, and Peter Williams, a white man born in Belgium in 1830. Cox was a cook on the Portland-based brig *Albion Cooper* and spent his time at sea. He'd long ago left his wife and their three children; she was living with another man and their own two children at the time of Cox's final journey. Williams first went to sea at age nine and had sailed the world by the time he reached age twenty-seven. He became acquainted with an Irish sailor named Thomas Fahy (perhaps Fahey), and the pair traveled to Portland in 1857 and joined the crew of the *Albion Cooper*. Under the command of Captain Daniel R. Humphrey of Yarmouth, they set sail from Portland on August 10, 1857.

The *Albion Cooper* was heading to the Caribbean, but trouble arose along the way that would forever change the lives of all aboard. Williams described the events of the voyage during his confession just prior to his execution. He said that the ship's second mate had treated Cox and himself "with great barbarity." After enduring the mate's cruelty day after day, Williams finally lost his temper and stabbed him. As punishment, he was placed in irons below deck. He said that the mate drove a nail into a beam and hung him from it by his wrists, his feet just touching the floor. This caused great pain, and he lost consciousness as a result. Cox had become "maddened to desperation" by the abuse as well and suggested to Williams that they kill the captain and crew and take the ship. The two men trusted only Williams's friend Fahy and took him into their confidence. Williams was illiterate (Cox may also have been), so they knew they would need Fahy—who was literate—to help them sail the ship once they took control.

Captain Humphrey was sleeping on deck and was the first to be killed, receiving multiple blows to his head by Williams's hatchet. They next sneaked up behind the cruel second mate and struck him on the back of his head. His cries brought the first mate out of his cabin. He, too, was attacked but was able to retreat to his cabin to live just a few minutes more before he was overtaken and killed by Williams. Williams then turned back to the second mate to finish him off with a few blows of his hatchet. One other seaman became a victim at this horrible scene. The murderous duo weighted the four bodies with iron and tossed them overboard to their watery graves. Fahy had not participated in the slaughter; he was scared for his life. He secretly documented the mutiny and murders and then sewed the document into the lining of his jacket in hopes that someone would eventually find it and bring the mutineers to justice.

Cox and Williams decided to abandon the *Albion Cooper*. They set it afire and, with Fahy, began their final journey in a smaller boat, hoping to find an island nearby. Within two days, they were rescued by a Philadelphia-based brig. They claimed to the captain that their vessel had accidentally burned and that they were the only survivors, but on his earliest opportunity, Fahy told the captain the truth of the matter and gave him the written accounting he'd sewn into his jacket. The captain at first played along with Cox and Williams, treating them with the kindness expected to be given to any poor souls rescued from the sea. But once he reached his Caribbean destination, he put Cox and Williams in chains for the journey back to Portland. Along the way home, Thomas Fahy died and was buried at sea.

News of the murder of Captain Humphrey and his officers had reached Portland before the accused men did, and a lynching party was being formed to seek vengeance. So Abraham Cox and Peter Williams had to be secretly transported to prison. Once tried, they were found guilty of mutiny and murder and sentenced to death by hanging.

The Munjoy Hill gallows had long ago been dismantled, and a new jail was under construction. Cox and Williams were sent to jail in Auburn, Maine, and their hangings were carried out there on a new large double gallows. Spectators began to gather the night before, filling the homes of the locals, and by late morning one newspaper reported the crowd at ten thousand. While awaiting their deaths, both men confessed their guilt; Williams pointed to the ropes and said, "I deserve the place….I killed the most of them—four of them. I have to answer to that." Ropes were then passed around their elbows, drawing their arms back as far as possible. Their wrists and ankles were strapped, black hoods pulled over their heads and nooses placed around their necks. At 11:35 a.m. on August 27, 1858, the trapdoor of the gallows was released, and the two fell together. Though one paper reported that the bodies were to be interred on Portland's Martin's Point, burial records for Eastern Cemetery indicate their bodies were interred there. Like Goodwin, Bird and Drew before them, the exact location of their graves is no longer known. A fascinating broadside was published soon after the executions. Entitled *Last Words of Peter Williams and Abraham Cox*, it provided details—in rhyming verses—of the confessions of the two men.

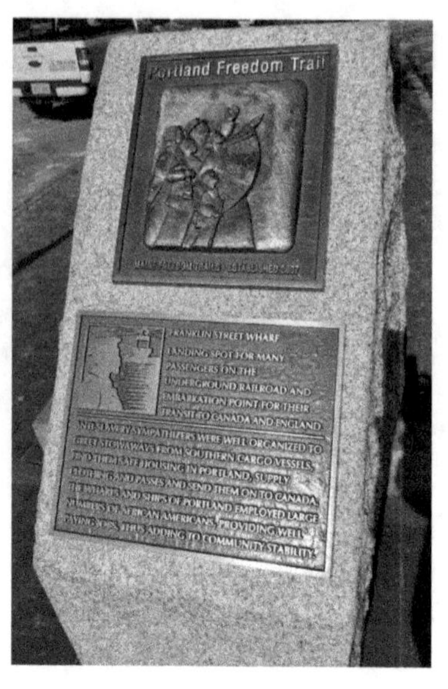

A Portland Freedom Trail marker on Portland's waterfront commemorating the efforts of many who helped escaped slaves reach freedom.

All sources seem to indicate that the cruelty Cox and Williams suffered came from one of the ship's mates and not the captain. The captain was indeed a good man, for on a journey that preceded the one in which he was killed, he had rescued a runaway slave from Savannah, Georgia. When discovering the stowaway aboard the *Albion Cooper*, he could have turned the slave in; not doing so put himself and his ship at great risk. Instead, upon reaching Portland, he secretly met with members of the antislavery network, who rescued the escaped slave and assisted in his escape to Quebec. Captain Humphrey is among the many honored for their courageous efforts with a Freedom Trail marker found today on Portland's waterfront.

It's not surprising that the locations of the graves of these five men are not known. Criminals were shunned; the townspeople wanted to forget about them. So it's likely that they were all buried in outlying areas of the Burying Ground without any markers to draw attention to their graves.

Chapter 7

AFRICAN AMERICANS

With a loaded pistol in hand, Richard L. Hill laid in wait for his father, Richard, at the home they shared on Munjoy Hill. It was September 13, 1861; the son was thirty-four; his father was seventy-three and a veteran of the War of 1812. Records describe them as "free colored persons" working as laborers who'd lived together for many years. Whatever was the root of their difficulties isn't clear, but when the elder Richard arrived home from work, his son fired a shot at him. Seeing that the bullet had left his father badly wounded and in great pain, he shot again "to put him out of misery." Two officers arrested him despite his claim of self-defense; he already had a robbery conviction to his name. His friends pleaded insanity on his behalf. The judge asked the jail's physician to observe him in order to determine sanity, but the report back to the judge left some doubt. The judge decided to commit him to the insane hospital until such time that the truth of his plea might be determined. Richard Hill (the father) was interred in an unmarked grave in the "North Yard" (Section A of the cemetery). Today, we find a marker from the Veterans Administration placed there in his honor.

There was little diversity on Portland Neck in the seventeenth and eighteenth centuries and no burial records kept, so we don't have clear proof that segregation of whites and nonwhites occurred within the burial ground in its earliest days. Practicality may have ruled the day, so that the bodies of the dead were simply put in whatever plots were easiest to dig on the hillside regardless of the color of their skin.

Segregation became clearer as the town developed and population increased. Likely the first such patch of land specially designated within the cemetery was the "Colored Ground" (now referred to as the "African American Ground") of Section L. By the end of the eighteenth century, people of color were relegated to the far back corner of the burial ground, in its easternmost point bordered today by Mountfort and Federal Streets. The first recorded African American placed there was Philip Acorn, age twenty-seven, who passed in 1797.

During the time that Eastern Cemetery was active, Portland's population of African Americans was never strong. But people of color had been coming as early as the whites had—just not as willingly. There were slaves in the area; in fact, not long ago, when the erection of a statue of Portland's first settler, George Cleeve, was being proposed, some locals expressed concerns about the city honoring a slave owner. Whether or not Cleeve brought a slave with him still seems to be unresolved. Regardless, Maine's landscape lacks the huge expanses of farmland (and has too short of a growing season) present in the South's plantations, where slaves were an integral part of the community. Here, early Africans were more likely servants to the wealthy.

In 1753, twenty-one slaves were counted in the Portland area. A local census taken in 1777 showed that Portland's population included "12 Negroes and 1 Mulatto." By 1783, Massachusetts had declared slavery illegal; Maine, being a district of Massachusetts at the time, followed this ruling. In the first U.S. census taken in 1790, residents were counted in categories of "free white" males and females, adult and underage. Of the 2,240 people in town, only 16 were categorized as "other free persons" (the "other" referring to nonwhites). For many years, Reverend Deane's journal documented new construction in town; among the buildings listed in 1799 were four "negro houses" erected by private landowners for the nonwhite members of their households.

THE FIRST "COLORED GROUND"

I examined the burial records in Jordan and other sources and found 264 people of color known to be buried at Eastern Cemetery. The true number is likely much larger, since so few good records exist for this population, and 70 percent of the known burials remain unmarked. Following Philip Acorn's interment in 1797, there is a gap of eighteen years in Section L records until

BILL OF MORTALITY.

The Sextons report the following number of deaths which have taken place in this town in the courſe of the laſt year ending December 31, 1807:—viz.

Grown perſons,		81
Children,		93
People of Colour,		9
Gaz.]	Total	193

The "Bill of Mortality," published in January 1808, showing the number of people who died in Portland in 1807.

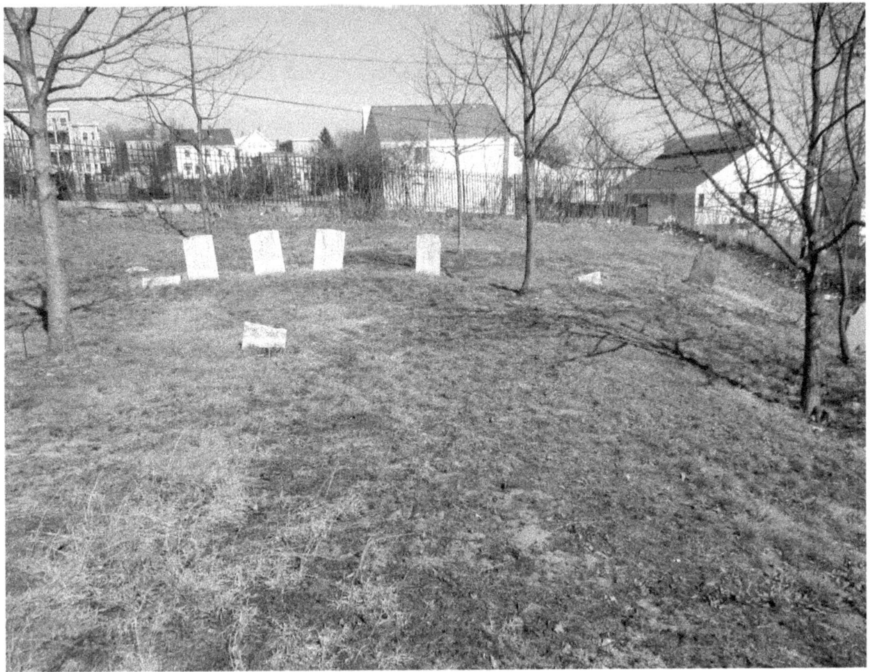

A current view of the first "Colored Ground," occupying the far northeast corner of the old section of the cemetery. Note the general lack of markers.

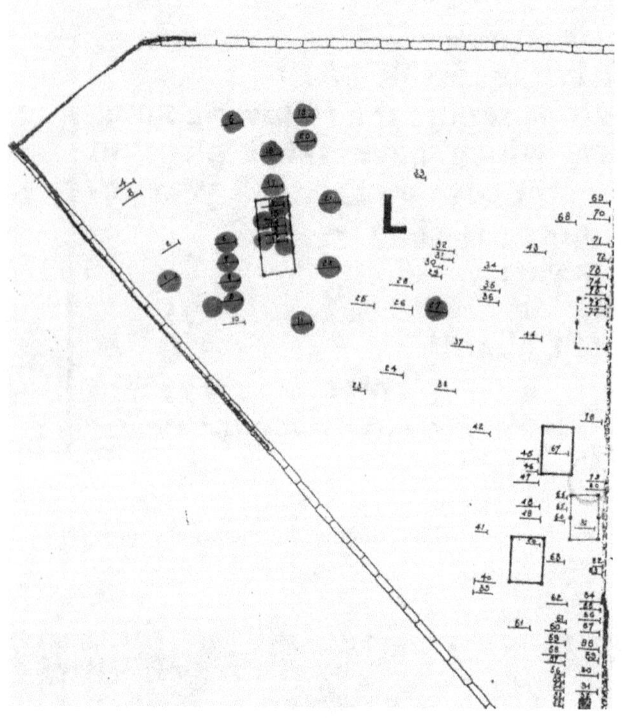

Graves of twenty known African Americans found in the old section (Section L), plotted on the 1890 survey map by the author. Each circle is a known grave. The other numbered graves within this section are quite likely occupied by African Americans.

the burial of Nancy Pier Manuel, age twenty-two, in 1815. She was the first wife of Christopher Christian Manuel (1781–1845), the first president of the Portland Union Anti-Slavery Society. But we know that people of color were buried in the intervening years, since annual vital statistics reported in the newspaper confirm this. In 1807, there were nine "people of colour" who passed in Portland and whose bodies likely were placed in the designated patch. The last confirmed burial in Section L was Eunice Shapleigh, who died at the age of seventy-six in 1869. Of the 85 confirmed graves for African Americans, 25 percent are found in the designated ground of Section L. Sadly, this area has been the subject of great neglect and vandalism over the years, and very few complete, readable markers remain.

The New Designated Patch

After the city purchased land from Reverend Smith (who was likely a slave owner himself, as he noted in his journal on November 16, 1774, "Our negro man, Jack, died"), another Colored Ground was established, and burials began there by 1825. This patch is located in today's front corner of the cemetery in Section A, at the intersection of Congress and Mountfort Streets. While now we find that section to be up front and facing our modern-day city's main thoroughfare, Congress Street, this was not the case when the designation was originally made. Congress was then called Back Street, upslope from the waterfront's center of activity, so the new designated patch was actually in the cemetery's far back corner. Of course, as explained in chapter 4, when the post-fire reconstruction work along the waterfront side of the burial ground was complete, the back of the cemetery became the front of the cemetery as it is today, and the African Americans buried in Section A now rest in a place of prominence: in clear view of all who pass by.

During the first half of the nineteenth century, the black community was growing; the maritime economy provided opportunities for whites and blacks alike, and free Africans made their way to Portland to find work on the waterfront, loading and unloading cargo from the multitude of trade ships coming to port. While some worked the docks, others took to the sea as sailors on trade ships or as servicemen during conflicts. The Abyssinian Meeting House, the first church for African Americans, was built in 1826. Its roof can be seen from the cemetery's Section L designated patch. It is within the city blocks nestled between the cemetery and the waterfront that became the heart of the African American community, where up to four hundred people of color lived and worked.

I found fifty-six confirmed burials for African Americans in the new patch, or about two-thirds of their total known graves. Their burials continued in Section A through the 1870s. Thankfully, a small collection of markers has survived the ages. Stones for mother and son Jannett C. Pear Ruby (1805–1827) and William Ruby (1825–1828) are found side by side. Jannett was the first wife of Reuben Ruby, a successful businessman, one of the founders of the Abyssinian Church and a leader in Portland's antislavery movement. Also there is the marker for Sophia L. Ruby Manuel (1802–1875), Reuben's sister. She was the second wife of Christopher Christian Manuel. The Manuels and Rubys were key players in Portland's Underground Railroad.

It should be no surprise that Portland played a role in the antislavery movement. Many free Portland-based African Americans went south on trade ships; others based in Portland moved goods off ships coming from the southern states. This provided great opportunity for the sharing of news about the conditions of southern blacks and the evolving views about enslavement itself as the proslavery and antislavery factions continued to dig

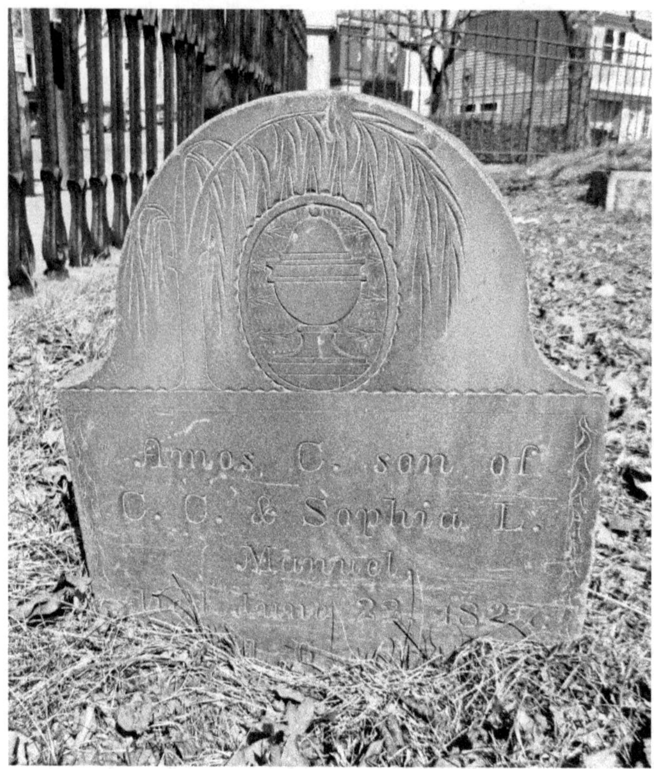

Left: The grave marker for Amos C. Manuel (died 1827) in the new "Colored Ground," established by about 1825. He was the son of Christopher and Sophia Manuel.

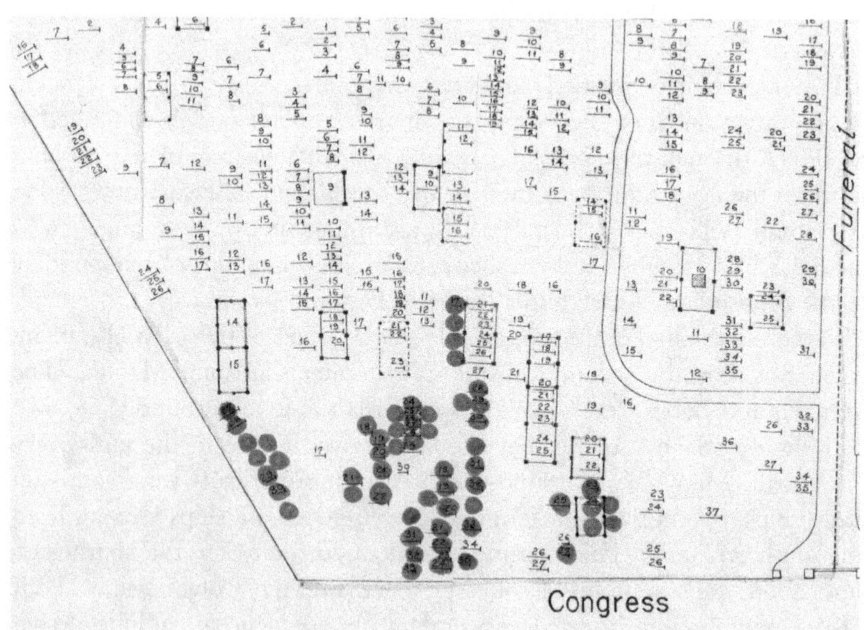

Below: Graves of fifty-six African Americans found in the new section (Section A), plotted on the 1890 survey map by the author. Each circle is a known grave.

deeper into their fundamental beliefs. Blacks and whites worked together in Portland to create a safe haven for escaping slaves, and Portland became a welcoming stop along the Underground Railroad. A fine self-guided walking tour brochure, *Portland Freedom Trail*, has been produced by the Portland Freedom Trail organization. It features locations of safe houses as well as Eastern Cemetery, and a marker is found outside the cemetery fence on Congress Street that honors the people who worked to help those who were fleeing slavery.

VETERANS' MONUMENTS

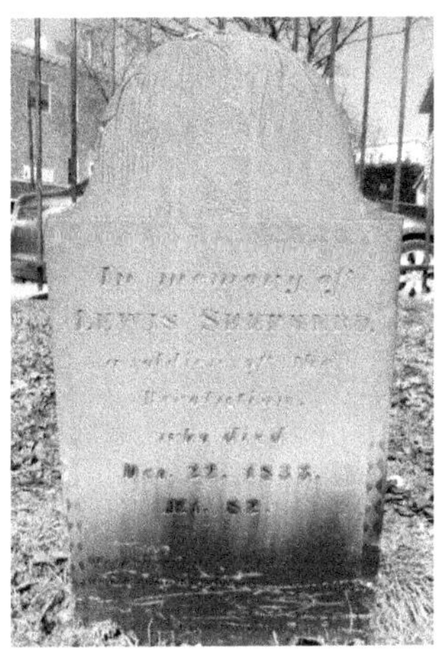

The original slate marker for African American Revolutionary War veteran Lewis Shepherd.

Five modern white marble markers supplied by the Veterans Administration are found in a row along the Mountfort Street fence in the Section A patch. They honor three black veterans who served in the Revolutionary War—James Bowes, Plato McLellan and Cato Shattuck; William "Billy" Brown, who served in the Quasi-War; and Richard Hill, the War of 1812 veteran who is profiled at the beginning of this chapter. In the same line is the original slate gravestone dated 1833 for African American Revolutionary War veteran Lewis Shepherd. As more African American veterans without markers are identified, additional stones may be placed in this line.

REACHING A "GOOD OLD AGE"

In reviewing the burial records for the cemetery's African Americans, I noticed the cause of death for one man was "good old age." James H. Samples, who passed in 1876, indeed reached the good old age of ninety-nine. A check of directories and census files revealed that Samples was born in Virginia in 1777. I believe he was born a slave, as I found a listing in a Virginia slaveholders' tax file that (if I am interpreting it correctly) indicates that he and his parents, Colvin and Sue, were "set at liberty" in 1779 by their owner, Captain William Douglas. Samples was in Maine by 1834 when he was listed in the directory as a mariner. He was a "handcartman" in 1841 and then, for the next two decades, a laborer. In his last entry—the 1870 U.S. census—he was in his nineties and living in a large household with the Clarks and Stevens, families whose names are also found among the blacks buried in the two designated patches. Like so many others, his grave is unmarked.

Chapter 8

FRIENDS

Loruhamah Howell waited thirty-five years for her husband to join her at Eastern Cemetery. She died in 1811 at the age of sixty, and her grave was adorned with a slate gravestone decorated with a simple urn carved by Bartlett Adams. Her husband, Silas, lived to one hundred and, when he died in 1846, was buried without a stone of his own. His death certificate notes cause of death as "old age," and his burial record notes he was "buried beside wife."

In 1795, town selectmen designated a portion of the burial ground for use by the Society of Friends, or Quakers. This "Friends' Ground," as it became known, is located near the Mountfort Street gate on Funeral Lane and holds the remains of thirty-one known Quakers. There are likely many more resting there in unmarked graves.

Reverend Smith wrote in his journal in 1743 that there were "several strange Quakers in town," suggesting that this group was not yet well understood. The Quakers were not living on Portland Neck in any great number but instead just west in Stroudwater (now part of Portland). Monthly Quaker meetings were established in 1751, and a meetinghouse was built in Stroudwater in 1752. Although the Friends followed their own religious beliefs, they were required to pay taxes to support a church they did not attend, the Congregational Church on the Neck. But in 1774, they were exempted from paying those taxes.

The first Quaker Meetinghouse on Portland Neck was constructed by 1796. It was a small building that Goold noted was made of brick, unusual for that time when the majority of structures were built of much more plentiful wood. He also noted that the Quaker Meetinghouse was the first house of worship in Portland that was warmed by a stove. It was "a large box-stove in the middle aisle, and covered with loose bricks, for any one to take to his seat for the warmth they held. The Quaker stove was the subject of ridicule, and several years passed before any other meetinghouse had one; but they all finally came to appreciate the warmth of a stove in church." Goold found that the diaries of Portland's other pastors included frequent mention of having to deal with frozen baptismal water in their unheated structures during wintertime services.

The Quakers generally lived a simple life, respectful of others and morally upright. Willis wrote that the first chief justice of Maine's Supreme Court, Prentiss Mellen, noted that in his forty-five years on the bench, he had known of only one criminal case involving a Quaker. Willis wrote, "This tribute from that able and experienced jurist is high commendation to the moral qualities of that worthy sect."

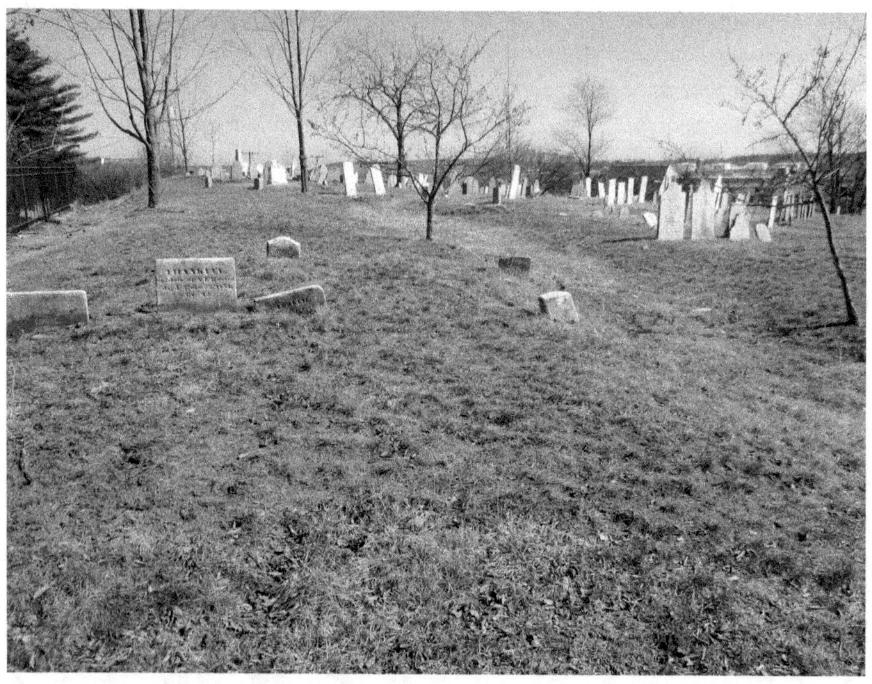

A current view of the Friends' Ground, just south of Funeral Lane near the Mountfort Street gate. Note the general lack of markers.

The Quakers were also opposed to hostilities of any kind. In the 1777 census taken to determine the number of males eligible to serve in the military (age sixteen or older), Quakers were specifically noted to be exempt from military duty. This presented some problems for the community during the American Revolution. Some Quakers—in their refusal to pay taxes to support the war effort—found their property taken from them. Others who did relax their scruples in order to assist in the War for Independence found themselves rebuked by the Society. I found a record of one Quaker who did serve in the Revolutionary War. Rufus Horton (circa 1759–1840) participated in the famous 1775 battle at Lexington, Massachusetts. His military record is found on the application by a descendant for admittance to the Sons of the American Revolution. Apparently, Horton's service was forgiven, for he was buried in the Friends' Ground when he passed away in 1840.

Quaker graves prior to 1800 were always left unmarked since the Friends prohibited public displays of wealth or social position at the time. But attitudes changed after the turn of the century for the simple fact that some Quakers wanted to know where loved ones had been buried. So grave markers began to be used, but they could not be elaborate. A name, date and age were acceptable, but no ornamentation, epitaphs or decorations were allowed, and the stones were limited in size and height. The earliest markers found within the Friends' Ground at Eastern Cemetery today bear this out. However, as the decades passed through the 1800s, markers became larger and more similar to all others being placed throughout the cemetery.

John Taber (1755–1811)

The earliest known marker in this section is for John Taber, who died in 1811. He came to Portland from the central Maine town of Vassalborough in 1796. He and his wife, Elizabeth (Wing) Taber, had by then thirteen children, at least three of whom had passed away before the family's move. He became a successful merchant after forming a business partnership with another Quaker, Samuel Hussey. Hussey controlled the activity at one of Portland's busier wharfs, allowing the company to prosper in its import and export of goods with Europe. Despite their success, the business did not last long, and John Taber brought his son Daniel into a new partnership, John Taber & Son, located on Union Wharf.

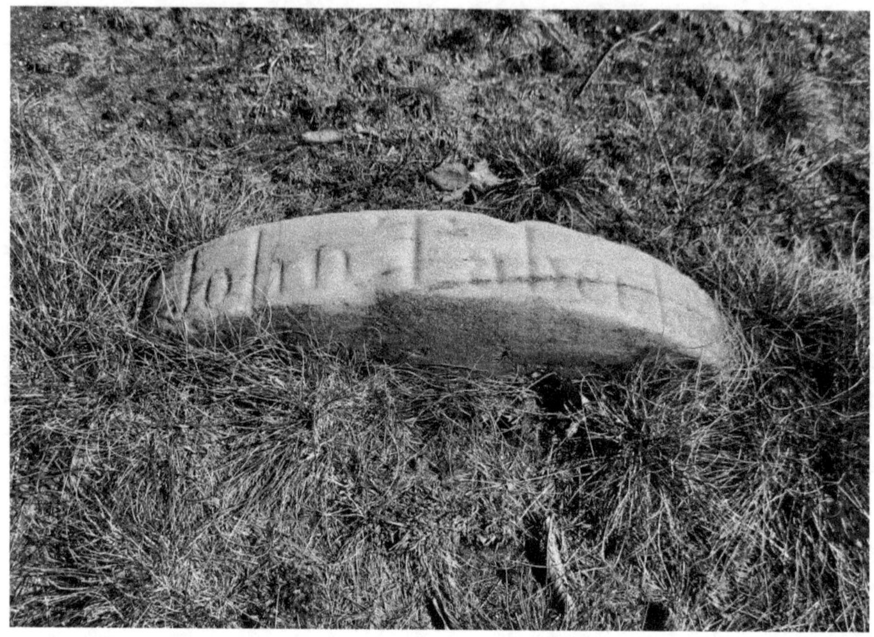

The marker carved for John Taber, a Quaker. Note its small size, lack of decoration and inscription on the stone's top edge.

That company was so successful, and the Tabers so trusted, that Taber & Son created a new moneymaking scheme for themselves that consisted of issuing paper currency that could be exchanged by the holder of the note for silver. Laws did not prohibit this at the time, and Taber & Son became an alternative to the two local banks. Many Portland businesses honored the Taber Notes; they'd accept them from customers who were buying their goods and then exchange them for cash from Taber & Son. Because the local economy was flooded with counterfeit currency, Taber Notes proved popular, and Taber & Son thrived. Daniel Taber may have taken advantage of their good fortune. Goold wrote that whenever Daniel needed money for his personal use, he'd simply print up more notes.

Unfortunately, with the onset of President Jefferson's trade embargo in 1807, the economy failed, and Taber Notes became worthless. Lawsuits followed from angry holders of the notes. Legislation came in 1809 that prohibited the issuance of currency by private banks. John Taber may have been rebuked by the Society of Friends for his failure, but he was allowed burial in the Friends' Ground. He was joined there by his wife in 1814 and at least three other members of the family.

The stones used to memorialize the graves of the Tabers are unique with respect to all other markers at Eastern Cemetery but not for Quaker gravestones found in other New England burial grounds. The Taber graves have short, thick, white marble stones buried so that only the top few inches of the marker are visible; the name is carved on the exposed top edge of the stone. When wandering through the cemetery, the Taber family stones can easily be overlooked or mistaken for footstones.

Mapping the Quaker Plots

The designated patch authorized in 1795 was an area of twenty-five square rods at the end of Funeral Lane on Mountfort Street. If truly a square-shaped plot, it would occupy a space of approximately eighty feet by eighty feet. But since the fence line along Mountfort Street runs at nearly a forty-five-degree angle to Funeral Lane, the designated burial area was more likely somewhat irregular. Past versions of the self-guided tour maps Spirits Alive provided to visitors indicated that the Friends' Ground was found north and south of Funeral Lane by the Mountfort Street gate. In an effort to confirm the location, I plotted the graves of known Quakers.

Burial notes for confirmed Quakers typically state, "Buried Quaker Lot," "Buried Quaker Ground" or "Buried Friends' Ground." Recorded burials in the Friends' Ground spanned six decades, from 1811 to 1873. In addition, notes exist for some who were buried nearby, such as "Buried near the Friends' Ground," "Buried east corner Friends' Ground" and "Buried at the head of the Friends' Ground." Whether these people were actually Quakers isn't clear, but their notes suggest that the boundary of the Quaker burial patch was well defined.

For those identified as Friends in Jordan's book, I cross-checked names with other sources (primarily published histories of Portland) to confirm they were in fact Quakers. Those sources also identified a few other Friends who had not been labeled as such in Jordan's research. In total, I found thirty-seven Quakers buried at Eastern Cemetery, the majority of whom are within the designated Friends' Ground.

Once the known graves were plotted, the picture became clear: the Friends' Ground is limited to the south side of the lane near the gate. No Quakers are buried on the north side of the lane, and that section of the cemetery is occupied by the Section A underground tombs anyway. Goold had written that the 1795 Friends' Ground was in "the northerly corner of the burying ground." At the time, the northerly corner ended where Funeral Lane now exists and would not have extended into Section A. As a result, our visitors' map now reflects that the Friends' Ground exists only in the old section, south of Funeral Lane and the gate.

OTHER QUAKERS IN THE FRIENDS' GROUND

Taber's early business partner, Samuel Hussey, was buried just a few paces away from him. William E. Gould wrote that following the economic bust, Hussey tried to settle a sixty-dollar debt owed to Taber using Taber Notes, but Taber refused them, admitting they were worthless. Hussey died in 1837, having lived eighty-two years. His wife, Thankful (Purinton) Hussey, also lived to a good old age; she passed in 1851 at the age of ninety-two. Their fourth of seven children, Miriam, is with them, too. She lived to age fifty-four and passed in 1844.

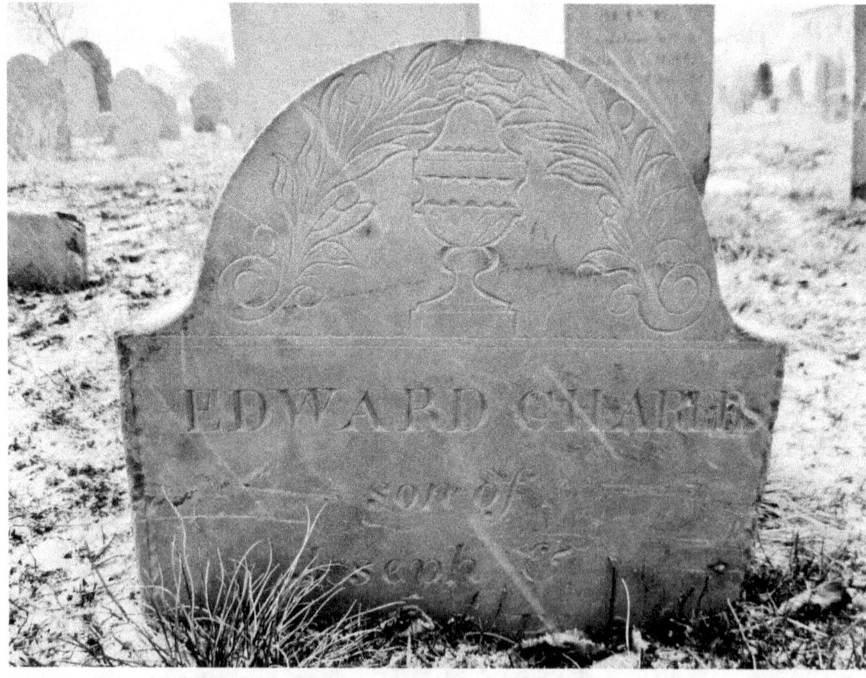

The slate marker from 1819 for two-year-old Edward Charles Pope. He and five other members of the family were buried in a lot outside the Friends' Ground.

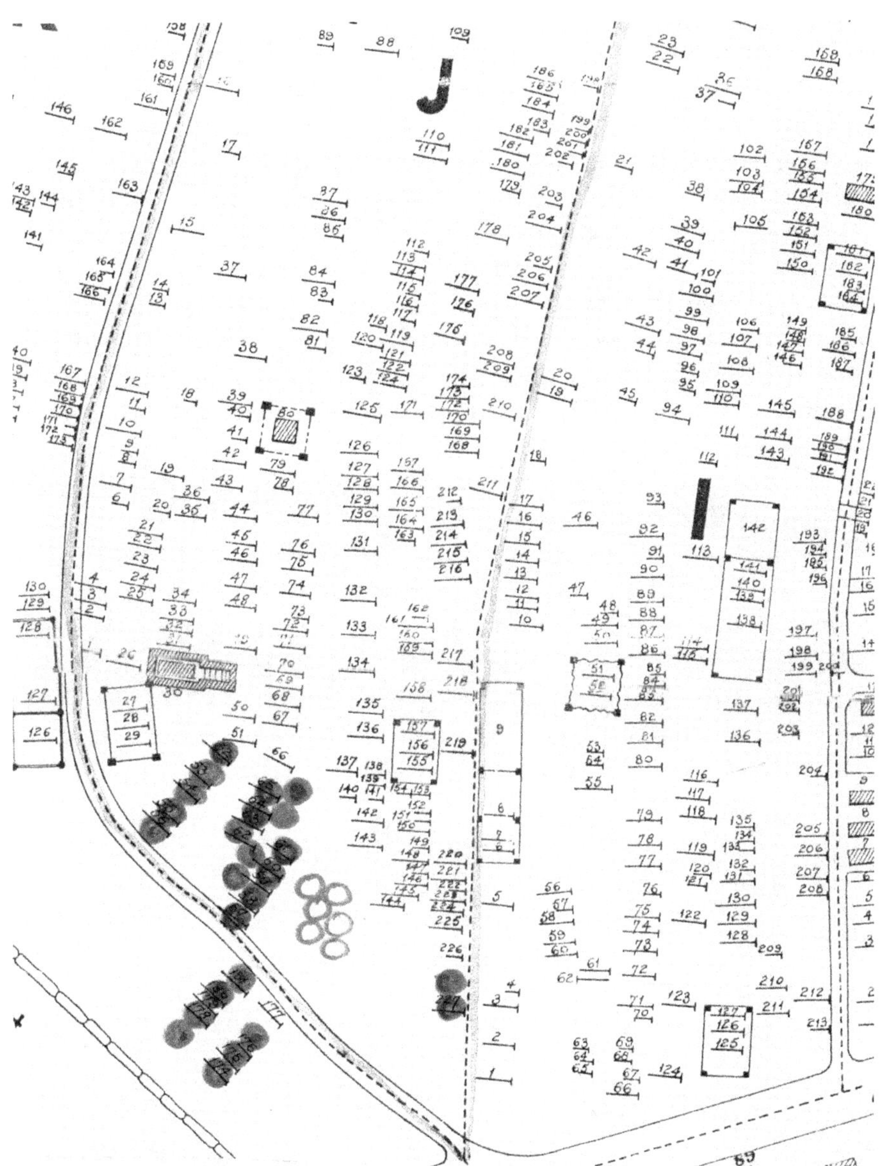

Graves of Quakers found in the Friends' Ground, plotted on the 1890 survey map by the author. Each solid circle is a confirmed grave location; the open circles represent unconfirmed locations of graves for six Quakers known to be somewhere within the Friends' Ground.

Other families found within the Friends' Ground are Pope (seven people), Poor (four people), Walker (four) and Horton (three). The Popes died between 1828 and 1841; six other Popes were buried in a family lot away from the patch, in Section F, closer to the center of the old section. Those burials occurred between 1815 and 1828, and my guess is that the Pope family owned the Section F plots prior to joining the Society of Friends.

Finally, I found two graves within the Friends' Ground for individuals whom I could not confirm were Quakers. Volunteer tour guide Anne Payson put me in touch with local expert Andy Grannell, who also was unable to confirm the two as Friends. Some Quaker burial grounds hold the remains of people who were not Quakers, and given the overcrowded conditions at Eastern Cemetery, it's Andy's hunch that the two unconfirmed Friends were "strays." For now, I simply note that Dorcas Baker (died 1830) and James Vanblarcom (died 1856) are in the Quaker lot.

The number of Quakers living on Portland Neck was never strong; Willis reported just nineteen people in the Society of Friends in 1864. In each of the decades from 1810 to 1840, I found just five or six Quaker burials. Three burials in the Friends' Ground are known in the 1850s, six in the 1860s and two in the 1870s. Within the designated patch, I calculated room for about one hundred additional bodies. Whether the unmarked places within the Quaker patch are occupied is a question left unanswered.

Chapter 9

STRANGERS

Orson Hemphill was one of a dozen children born to Joseph and Susanna Hemphill, who lived in New Hampshire, due west of Portland about one hundred miles. Orson's slate gravestone at plot B-6-23 explains the irony of his death at age twenty-six on September 14, 1826. It reads, "Died in this town while on a visit for his health."

When we think about the development of the cemetery during the town's population increase and diversification, it's clear that designated patches were established for minority groups along the outer edges of the burial ground, while the majority—white Protestants—were occupying the individual plots and family lots of the open ground.

In September 1766, Reverend Smith wrote, "The town is full of strangers." Trade ships were common in the bustling port, and immigration was on the rise. When one of these visitors died, the town was responsible for burying the body. When a corpse washed ashore, a homeless person was found dead or a friendless person perished, the town needed a place to bury their remains. Some communities set off special sections called potter's fields, paupers' graves or common grounds. At Eastern Cemetery, smaller, unclaimed sections of the open ground were set off as "Strangers' Grounds." Jordan wrote, "More than one such section was apparently so designated… unfortunately the location of these sections in now unknown." I took that as a direct challenge from Mr. Jordan and began my next adventure—the search for the Strangers' Grounds!

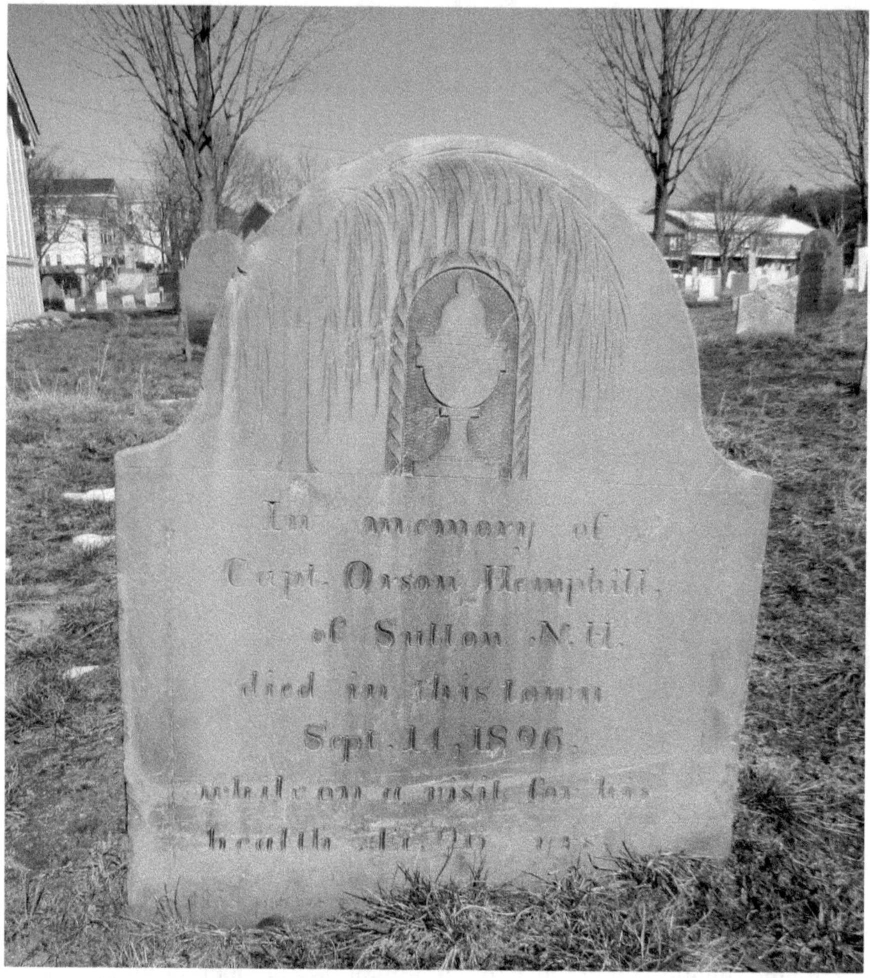

The grave marker for Captain Orson Hemphill, who died in 1826. Note the bottom of the inscription, that he died "while on a visit for his health."

The starting point for this task was to examine the burial records. I found records for four unknown children buried in unrecorded plots: a four-month-old illegitimate female found in 1844, a seven-week-old found at the back of Munjoy Hill in 1855, a two-day-old born at sea aboard an English steamship in 1858 and a child found in Portland Harbor in February 1863 whose body was stored in the Receiving Tomb.

There were also records for seven unknown adults. They died between 1842 and 1869 and consisted of three who drowned, a Catholic found murdered, remains unearthed during excavation at Fish Point, one who died aboard a steamer from Newfoundland and a twenty-three-year-old seaman who died from a fall. Six were buried in unrecorded plots. But the seventh—a man found drowned in 1848—provided the first clue in finding the Strangers' Grounds. His record noted he was buried in the Strangers' Ground "near the gate." While this clue was not a slam-dunk, it did suggest a Strangers' Ground exists near the Congress Street entrance.

A STRANGERS' GROUND IS FOUND

I found eighteen records for named individuals that specifically mentioned burial in the Strangers' Ground (one of these used the word "Foreigner" instead of "Stranger"). More clues were found in these records.

James W. Noyes, age two, and his mother, Mary Noyes, age thirty-three, were buried next to each other in 1846. Mary died of smallpox on August 15; James died six days later of intestinal illness. A heavily eroded stone is found for them in Section A, row 5, plots 23 and 24. These two plots are very close to the Congress Street gate, likely within the same patch where

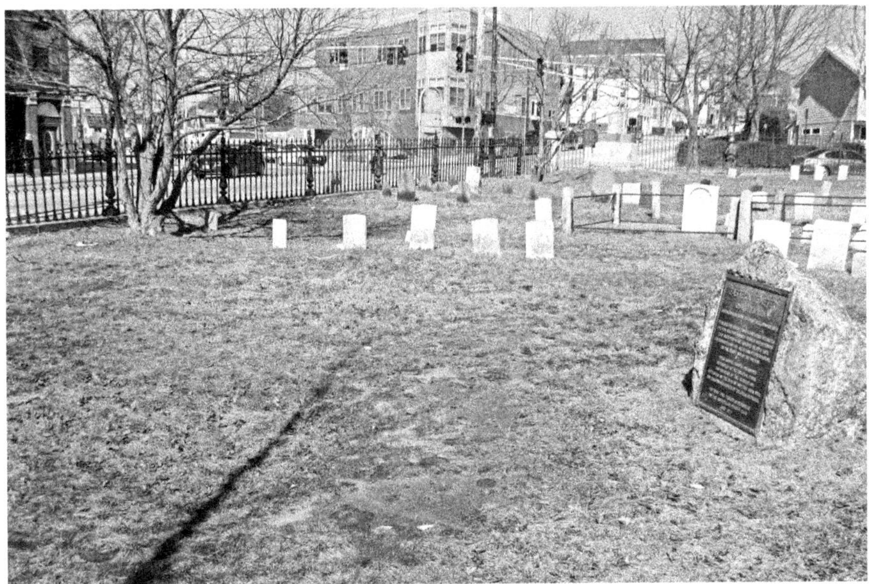

This open patch just inside the front gate was the site of the Hearse House (no longer there) and one of at least two Strangers' Grounds used for burial of the friendless, poor and unknown. The eroded marble Noyes stone is to the left, just out of view.

the drowned man's body lies. The next clue came from the record for John Nichols, a sailor aged twenty-two, who died of fever in 1844. Nichols was buried in the Strangers' Ground "near [the] Hearse House door."

In the early days, people transported bodies by their own means to the cemetery. But by 1805, the town had a horse-drawn hearse that was used to pick up the deceased and bring them to the cemetery for burial. A garage was built, called the Hearse House, and it stood across Funeral Lane from where the Dead House stands today. A boulder bearing a commemorative plaque is now found on the approximate site of the Hearse House, and a look at the Goodwin plot map confirms that this is a relatively open patch that includes the Noyes stones but few others. The location fits a familiar pattern: the town used the land along the outer edges of the cemetery for burial of those outside the majority class. With the Noyes pair, Mr. Nichols and the drowned man all there, it was an easy conclusion for me to reach—that a Strangers' Ground is there.

A SECOND IS IDENTIFIED, A THIRD IS LIKELY

Clues to a second Strangers' Ground are found within the records for two members of the Williams family. Nelson Williams died of unknown causes in 1837 at age seventeen. His sister Harriet followed him in 1843, when she died at age twenty of typhus fever. They share a white marble gravestone at plot G-24, and their records note that they were buried in the Strangers' Ground. In visiting the site, I found that there is a small open patch of ground adjacent to their graves straddling the border between Sections G and H that could hold about twenty other people. This must be a second Strangers' Ground.

Two markers for foreigners provide the possibility of a third Strangers' Ground. The 1848 marker for Cosmo de Sanchez (from Mexico) and the 1824 marker for Gabriel La Fogue (from Hispaniola) are within steps of each other straddling the line between Sections B and C. The fact that these two foreigners were buried so close together on the outer edge of the cemetery suggests the possibility of a third patch for strangers. Other burials in this patch are currently being studied and may lead to the naming of a third Strangers' Ground.

Jordan found that in 1838, the town decided to allow burial of two strangers per plot (one stacked on the other). Around this time, overcrowding

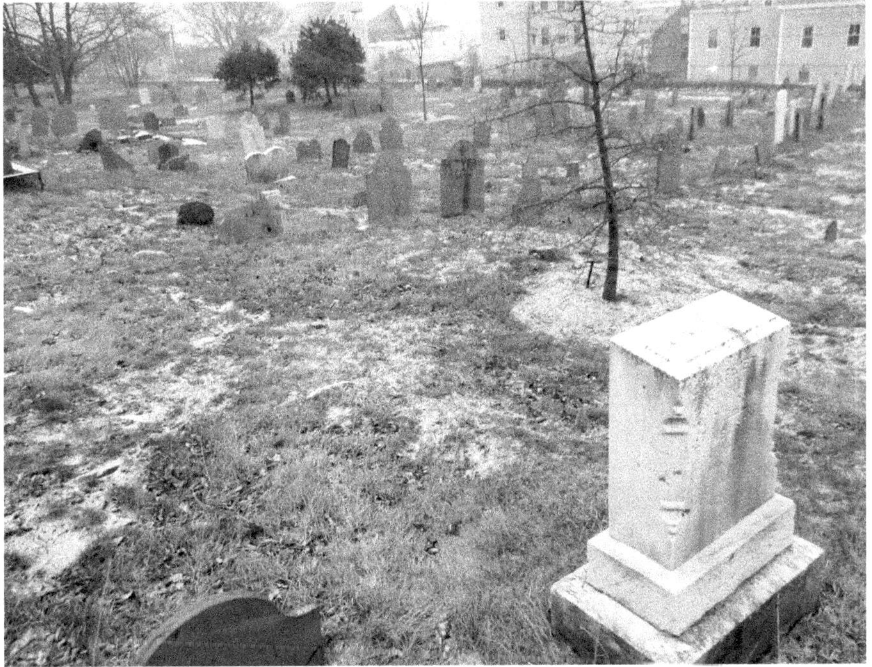

The marble marker for Nelson and Harriet Williams is in the lower right of the photo on the edge of the second known Strangers' Ground, the small open patch of ground just behind.

of the cemetery was at its peak, so this decision helped ease the pressure to find any of the few remaining unoccupied plots.

In all, I found twenty-eight people with references to being buried in the Strangers' Grounds. But clearly there are many more, for these are the people who would not have had family to erect a monument on their behalf. For now, we know where at least two of their designated patches are located, and our visitors' map has been updated accordingly.

ONE WELL-KNOWN STRANGER

One man received a handsome marble stone when he died in 1842. James Bannatyne was visiting from Scotland and had been lecturing in Portland on the subject of the evils of drinking alcohol. There was a more universal temperance movement underway, but Portland would soon famously become ground zero in the effort. Public lectures alone couldn't solve the problem of drunkenness, and Portland's mayor, Neal Dow, decided to attack the issue legislatively. In 1851, Maine became the first "dry state." Dow ultimately ran unsuccessfully for U.S. president in 1880, representing the Prohibition Party.

Bannatyne's lecture at the Park Street Church in July 1842 proved so popular that he was asked to repeat it the following week at the First Parish Church. Soon after, it was published with the title "Intemperance Among Literary Men: An Address Delivered Before the Portland Young Men's Total Abstinence Society…" He said:

> *There are some vices so immediately and so terribly ruinous, that our censure of the immorality is almost lost in our commiseration of the suffering. And one of these is the vice of habitual intemperance, which is, in truth, a protracted suicide—an incessant war waged by man against himself, against his own happiness, against all his interests, both of body and of soul. He is punished almost in the act of transgression, and more severely punished at each repetition of the act, till at length misery—unmitigated misery—becomes his daily and hourly portion.*

Although Bannatyne's Portland vital record indicates that he was taken down by consumption (tuberculosis) at age forty, the marker carved in his honor notes his age as thirty-four. Regardless, embalming had not yet been perfected, so it was impossible to return his body to Scotland. His marker was supplied by the Young Men's Temperance Society and reads:

A STRANGER'S GRAVE

James Bannatyne
Scotia's Gifted Child
A man of rare worth
in Simplicity, Gentleness,
Natural Talents,
Sound Development,
and of Eloquence
unsurpassed.
Died
Oct 29, 1842.
Æt. 34.
Erected by the Young Men's Temperance Society

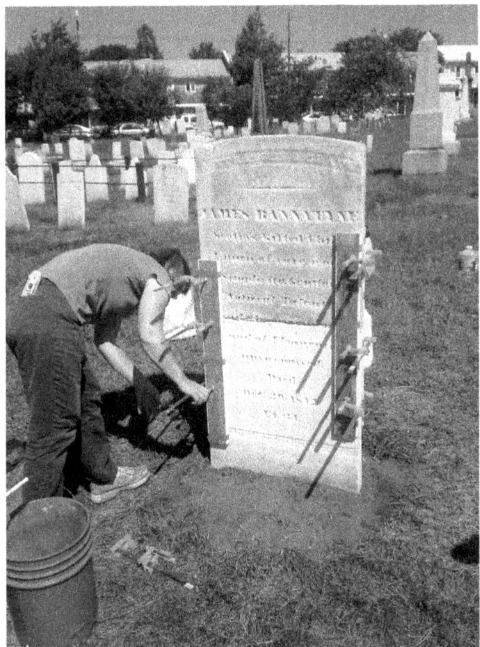

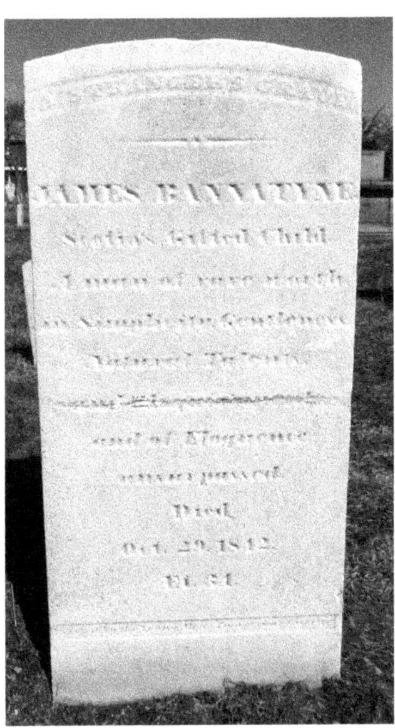

Left: Conservator Martha Zimicki repairing the marker for James Bannatyne. *Courtesy of Janet Alexander.*

Right: The marker for James Bannatyne after conservation by Spirits Alive.

Bannatyne's marker—like so many others—broke long ago and lay neglected on the ground. In 2014, the Spirits Alive conservation crew repaired and cleaned his stone, and today it stands tall for all to see at plot A-7-1.

Chapter 10

DISCOVERY OF THE CATHOLIC GROUNDS

Captain Samuel McLellan committed suicide on May 14, 1854, at the age of fifty-nine. He had been listed as a shipmaster in Portland's directories for more than twenty years and had been married to Eliza Jones for twenty-seven. The McLellans were a large clan, well-known and well-to-do. They'd been burying family in Tomb A-86 for many years before the captain took his own life; nine were already entombed there when the captain's body was interred, and five more would follow him in the years to come.

Angela Dexter, a Spirits Alive volunteer tour guide, posed a question one day while exploring the cemetery: "Was there a designated Catholic section?" I didn't recall ever seeing anything written about a Catholic ground at Eastern Cemetery and thought that if there was a designated patch, some earlier historian would surely have documented it. Still, I didn't have a definitive answer but promised to find out.

English Protestants were our earliest settlers, but we know that African Americans and Quakers were part of the fabric of the community too. Irish Catholics made their way here as well, some as indentured servants and others as free people in search of a better life.

Irish Catholics in Portland

Matthew Jude Barker has written a fine book on this subject (*The Irish of Portland, Maine*). He noted that the first known Irish settler was Thaddeus Clarke, who arrived around 1660 and occupied land on the peninsula until he was killed by natives in 1690. He wrote that many more Irish settled in the area by the 1730s:

> *These Irish people, due to the lack of Catholic priests, were married by and had their children christened by the local Protestant ministers. They were wise to lie low, as anti-Catholicism was rampant at the time. Irish Catholics were called "St. Patrick's vermin" by the Puritans, and Catholic priests and masses were outlawed by the Massachusetts Bay Colony.*

By the early 1800s, there was a community of Irish Catholics in Portland. The *Portland City Guide* noted that baptisms occurred in 1811, 1812 and 1815 by a visiting priest. By 1822, there were forty-three Catholics in Portland, and they petitioned the region's bishop for their own local parish. Just five years later, according to Barker's research, there were 120 to 130 Catholics in town. In order to serve the growing population, construction of the first Catholic church began in Portland in 1828. The first official Holy Mass was offered at St. Dominic's Church in the fall of 1830, with a parish of about 300.

The opening of Portland's first Catholic church occurred about the same time as the opening of Western Cemetery on Bramhall Hill. Eastern Cemetery was rapidly filling, so Western Cemetery offered relief to the problem of lack of burial space. With Irish Catholics on the increase, it's no coincidence that a special section of Western Cemetery was consecrated as the "Catholic Ground." In the collections of the Maine Historical Society (MHS), we find rosters of Irish Americans buried at both cemeteries. The Catholic Ground at Western Cemetery received over 1,300 people, primarily between 1840 and 1870.

Before long, the Catholic Church desired its own cemetery to serve the Catholics of the area, and so a large tract of land in South Portland was purchased in 1858 for this purpose. Calvary Cemetery was quickly developed and consecrated and began to receive the remains of Catholics. It was not uncommon in the nineteenth century for families to move human remains from one place to another, and so both Eastern and Western Cemeteries experienced a loss of some Irish Catholic subterranean residents once Calvary opened.

The Irish population had not yet blossomed in Portland during the time that Eastern Cemetery was most active, so the list of Catholics buried at Eastern contains far fewer names than the list for Western Cemetery. And the number, though small, is not exact. The roster (created circa 2000) lists fifty people.

In Jordan's book, burial records include the notation of "Catholic" for those people known to be so. I did a page-by-page review of his list and found forty-nine designations of Catholic, the majority of which matched the MHS roster, as expected. I found that Matt Barker's book contained another dozen Catholics who were not on the MHS roster or who were listed in the Jordan book but without the designation of Catholic. Finally, I spent some time researching the early known Portland Catholic families using vital records, census records and family trees. Some new family members of known Catholics were found and then confirmed to be buried at Eastern Cemetery. In all, I was able to bump the list up to seventy-eight Catholics buried at Eastern Cemetery.

THE EARLIEST CATHOLIC BURIALS

Records for burials within Eastern Cemetery were not well maintained until 1795, so it is very likely some Irish Catholics were interred in the 1700s. Nineteen-year-old John Mayland, "a native of Ireland," is the earliest known Catholic interment at Eastern, but his 1804 record does not actually state he was Catholic, his gravestone is missing and his plot location within the burial ground is unknown. So most sources rely on the first recorded Catholic burial to be that of Mary Gannen in 1807. She was twenty-nine at the time of her death, listed as a Catholic and her gravestone has survived.

Her small slate marker is quite interesting, with a design that is entirely unique. It features a rustic Holy Cross with a pair of bones crossed underneath. While crossed bones and skulls were sometimes carved on markers in the 1700s, those designs were largely out of style by the time she died. I have attributed the marker to stonecutter Robert Hope, who was working in the Adams shop at the time. It is the only one of its type I've found during my extensive surveys of his work.

The only other marker from the Adams shop I've found featuring a Holy Cross (but without crossed bones) is also located at Eastern Cemetery. It's for James Davis, who died in 1810 at age forty-six. This marker was carved by

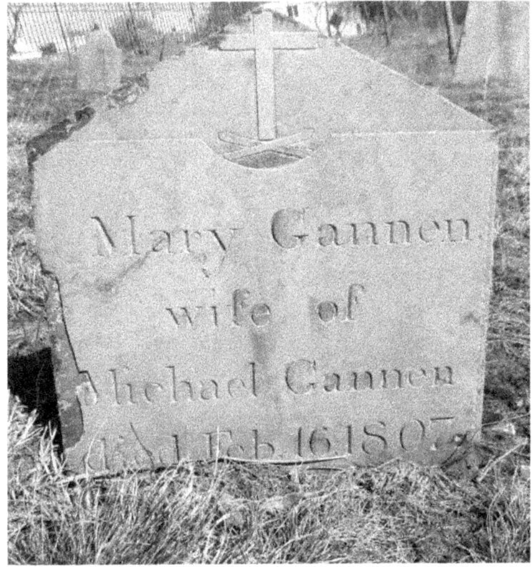

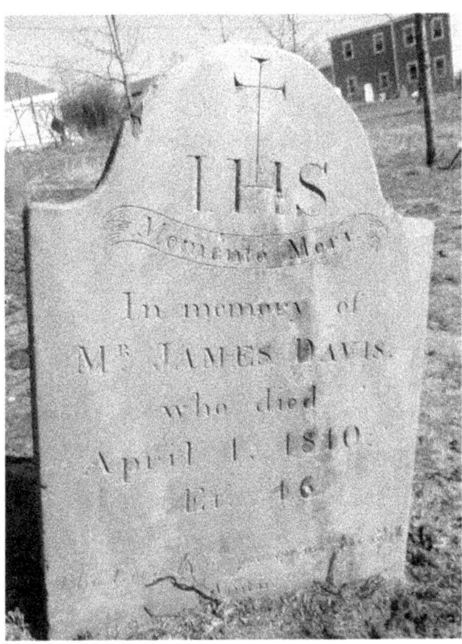

Left: The grave marker for Mary Gannen (died 1807). This is the only known stone produced in the Adams shop to feature a Holy Cross and bones.

Right: The grave marker for James Davis (died 1810). Carved by Bartlett Adams, this marker features a cross and uses both English and Latin.

Bartlett Adams himself. While Jordan indicated Davis's stone had been lost, I found it very near to the Gannen stone. It's a slate that features a simple Holy Cross and the letters "I.H.S.," Latin for *Iesus hominum Salvator*, or "Jesus, the savior of humankind." In slang, IHS is referred to as "In His Service."

Under this design, instead of crossed bones we find a banner with the Latin *Memento Mori* ("remember death" or "remember we must die"). Bartlett knew Latin and used it on a good number of markers, including the three that he carved for his own infant children. The Gannen and Davis markers are found in Section L, near the designated ground for African Americans.

Given the age of the cemetery and the many years of neglect, vandalism and natural deterioration of the place, it's no surprise that so many grave markers are missing and so many grave locations unknown. Only about one-third of the known graves in the entire cemetery today are marked with gravestones. This holds true for Catholics. Of the seventy-eight Catholics, forty-eight have known plot locations and just twenty-eight of those have markers on their graves. Thirty Catholics rest in plots without known locations.

A DESIGNATED PATCH FOR CATHOLICS

I plotted the known graves on the map to see if a pattern could be found. As noted previously, the first two Catholic burials were in the far back of the cemetery. One more grave from 1822 is found there—for Mary Martin, an African American Catholic, who died at age forty-two. Her stone is badly damaged, and just a fragment is left. Her husband was Francis Martin, whose record notes he was black and Catholic. His slate grave marker has survived among a cluster of nine Catholic gravestones in Section A. Those graves abut (or are within) the second, newer, African American designated ground of the cemetery. Francis died fourteen years after his wife, in 1836. The fact that he was buried in the new section and not by Mary's side in the old section suggests that Section L had completely filled up between 1822 and 1836.

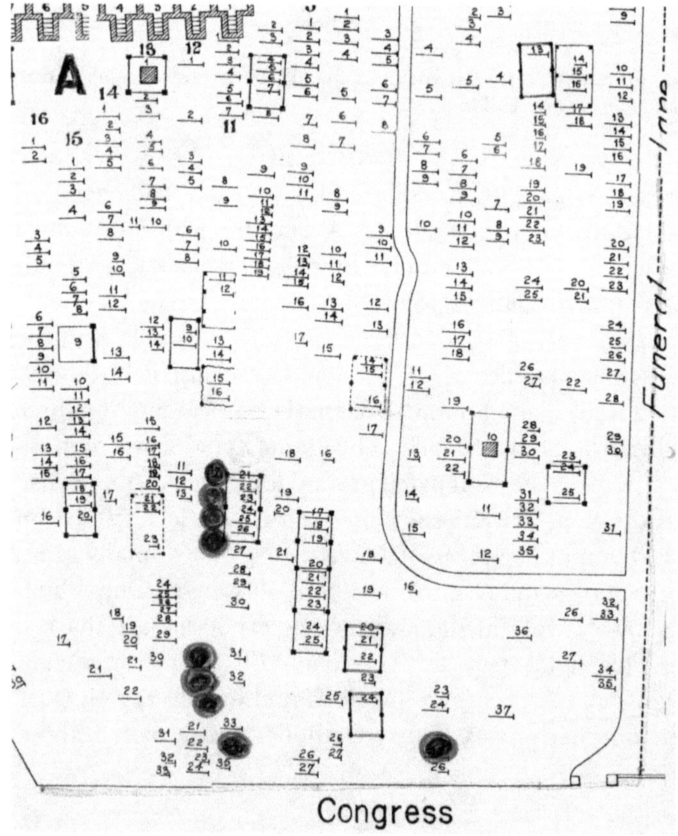

The graves of nine Catholics found in Section A, plotted on the 1890 survey map by the author. Eight of the nine are African Americans. Each circle is a known grave.

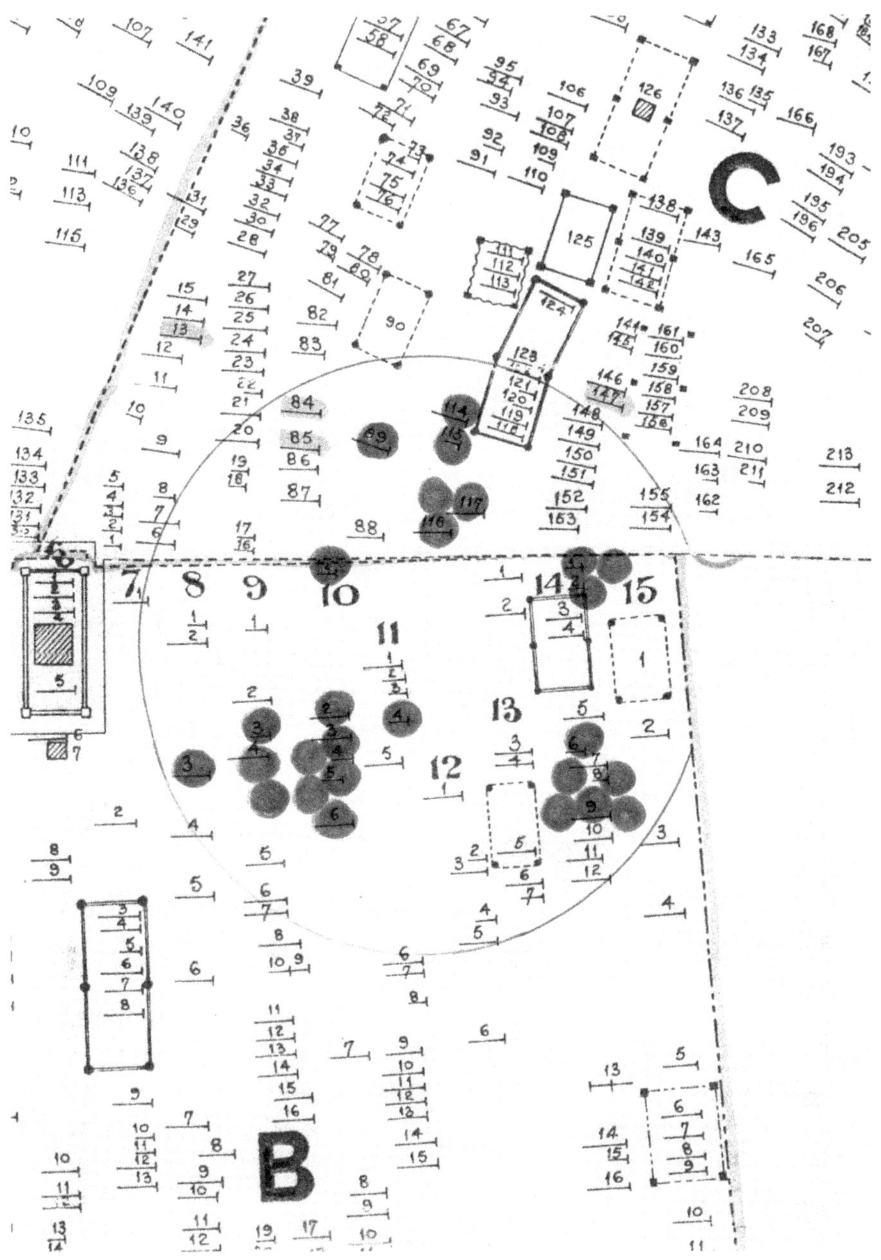

The graves of Catholics found in the new section (Sections B and C), plotted on the 1890 survey map by the author. Each circle is a known grave.

There are twenty-seven Catholic graves clustered on the borderline between Sections B and C. This represents 60 percent of the total known Catholic graves. Fourteen families are represented there. Seeing those graves plotted on the map creates a striking image that certainly suggests there was a patch of land designated for the burial of Portland's Catholics.

I shared my findings about this cluster of Catholic graves with Matt Barker and asked him about the possibility that this was an officially designated Catholic section. He has not found record of the consecration of any ground at Eastern Cemetery, though it's well known that consecrated ground was established at the newer Western Cemetery. Catholicism expert Lenny Telesca believes that the individual graves at Eastern Cemetery were most likely blessed by a priest (if present) at the time of burial but that the larger patch of land within which those graves lie would not have been consecrated by the Church since it was city, not Church, property. This makes sense because we also find burials of people who likely weren't Catholic within the same patch.

Only two other Catholics have known plots, and they are outside the circled patch shown on the map. John and Mary Woods died in 1835 at ages three and one, respectively. They share a gravestone, which is located in the center of Section B, not far from the designated patch. In consecrated grounds, people who committed suicide, were criminals or were excommunicated by the church were usually buried in outlying areas, often in unmarked graves. None of those seem to apply to these children, so their burial away from the others remains a mystery.

Within the circled area there is a wide range of death dates for Catholics—1813 to 1875—with most people being buried in the 1830s. There are thirty-five other graves within the same patch occupied by people who have not yet been identified as Catholic. The date range is similar—1808 to 1875—with the majority of burials occurring in the 1820s. Perhaps some of these people actually were Catholic, but their names just don't appear on any list, or perhaps this section simply contains a mix of Catholic and non-Catholic people because of the overall lack of available space at the time. I supplied a list of the questionable family names to Matt Barker, but he found none of them to be among the early Catholic families known to him.

Catholic Markers

There are twenty-eight gravestones for Catholics that can be found today at Eastern Cemetery: twenty are slate and eight are marble. Three stones are unreadable—the Mary Martin marker discussed above, a slate for Edward Shea (1824) that is broken down to the ground and a white marble marker for Nicholas Shea (1875) that is heavily eroded. Only a slate footstone survives on the grave of Henry McAnelley. But the remainder of markers are legible. Some stones are for a single person; others memorialize up to four members of a family.

Twenty markers are decorated with Catholic symbols. A simple Holy Cross and the letters "I.H.S." are most common. Four markers that were obviously cut by the same stonecutter also feature a heart. The heart can be found on non-Catholic stones as well and usually signifies love, but on these Catholic stones, we believe the heart to mean "love of Christ." Oddly, one of these was cut with the heart upside-down.

I asked gravestone symbolism expert Laurel Gabel about a possible meaning of the upside-down heart. She has rarely seen such a rendition,

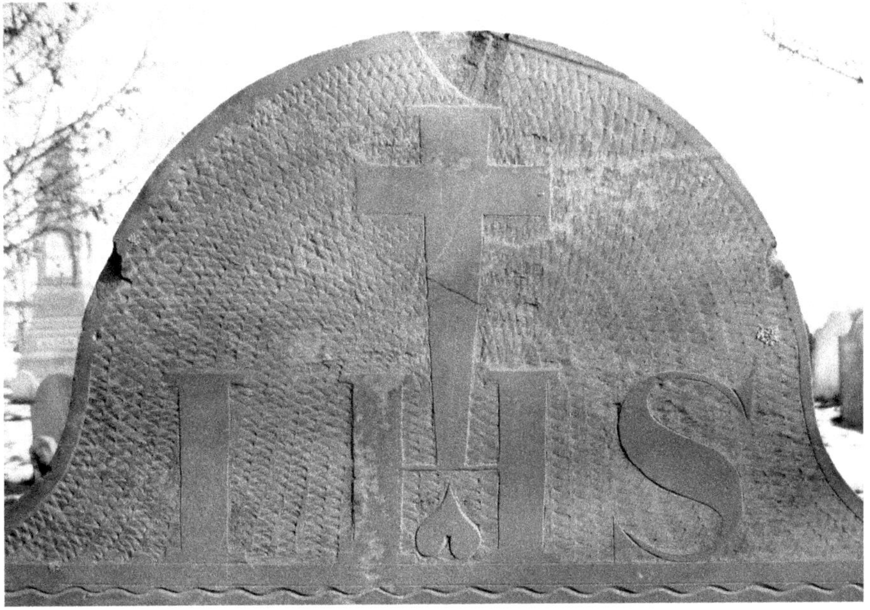

Detail of the 1837 marker for the Sherredon family, featuring a heart that was carved upside-down. Three other markers cut by the same stonecutter are found in Eastern Cemetery with hearts carved right-side-up.

and the meaning eludes her. Other gravestone enthusiasts suggest "death" or "the heart of the soul." Some wonder if this was simply the carver's error. I've found a few other upside-down hearts carved on grave markers, so I don't think this is a case of carver error. Instead, I believe there is a special meaning to this particular icon, and I continue to discuss possibilities with fellow taphophiles.

AFRICAN AMERICAN CATHOLICS

Six Catholics in Jordan also contain the note "Black." One of those is Mary Ann Syms, who died in 1848 at age forty-seven. She was buried in Section A. Four children named Syms are memorialized on a stone located in the same row. The children died between 1824 and 1839, years that Mary Ann Syms would have likely been able to bear children. The children's records are incomplete, since no ages are given, and a check of Portland vital records was of no additional help. Jordan does not list these children as black, but I added them to the list of African American Catholics based on my findings.

Of the ten known African American Catholics at Eastern Cemetery, eight were buried in the designated African American patch of Section A. Mary Martin was buried in Section L, as noted previously. Mary Ann Holland's location is unknown, although two other Holland graves are next to each other in Section A, leading me to believe that she, too, was buried there in 1844.

CAUSES OF DEATH

Almost half of the seventy-eight Catholics at Eastern Cemetery died in infancy or childhood; thirty-three died before age fifteen. Just two lived into their eighties. On very rare occasions, the cause of one's death is noted on the grave marker itself. This is not the case for our Catholics with grave markers. However, a check of Portland vital records and other sources helps reveal what brought these folks to the ends of their lives. Among the causes noted were consumption (tuberculosis), drowning, exhaustion, poisoning, scarlet fever and typhoid fever.

Conclusions

No formal designation has yet been discovered, and no evidence of consecration of any part of Eastern Cemetery is known. But given that there are two distinct clusters of graves within the cemetery holding the remains of 80 percent of the known Catholics, it's clear that segregation of Catholics occurred at the time of burial.

Recall that at the beginning of the nineteenth century, Irish Catholics (like African Americans) were often treated as second-class citizens. In fact, the burial locations of the Catholics and African Americans overlap in Section A of the cemetery. There seems to be no coincidence that the two earliest white Catholics (Gannen and Davis) were interred in the far back corner of the old section by the original African American designated ground.

Further, note that during the same period of time that at least twenty-seven Catholics—the largest cluster—were buried in Section B, we find the second-largest cluster (eight black Catholics) buried in Section A. The pattern seems clear—not only were Catholics separated from Protestants, but black Catholics were separated from white Catholics. The Spirits Alive visitors' map now includes the two designated Catholic sections to honor those Catholics who had in the past been forgotten. (Thank you, Angela, for asking!)

CHAPTER II

LOST AT SEA

Captain Benjamin Fenley was buried at sea. He was a single young man, just twenty-eight, who'd chosen a maritime life. In 1854, he was aboard a steamship that had left Panama with more than seven hundred traveling to New York City. But Captain Fenley wasn't piloting this ship; he was one of its many passengers. The steamer arrived in New York on September 27, a week after he'd been delivered to his watery grave. A monument was erected at Eastern Cemetery in his honor at location J-134. When his mother died many years later, she was buried beside her son's cenotaph.

Burial records for Eastern Cemetery reflect Portland's maritime economy. I found records for nearly two hundred men buried or memorialized who hold the title of captain, and while a few of those were the leaders of land-based regiments during the wars, the vast majority on the roster are sea captains.

Some of these men lost their lives at sea during battle. Others were taken by disease or accidental injuries or were washed overboard during storms. Captain Jacob Adams was lost off Cape Elizabeth in the 1807 wreck of the schooner *Charles*. There are four extraordinary grave markers from the shop of Bartlett Adams found today that memorialize the victims of the wreck. The complete details of the loss of the sixteen people aboard his ship are told in my first book, so I only note the tragedy here.

An examination of Jordan's records reveals the following burials and memorials at Eastern Cemetery:

- Sixteen were "drowned," "drowned at sea" or "drowned during passage."
- Fifteen "died at sea" or "died on passage." Four of these involve specific accidents; one other gives a cause of death of consumption.
- Ten were "lost at sea" or "lost overboard."
- Six were lost during battle at sea.
- One was shipwrecked (Captain Adams).
- One was "buried at sea" (Captain Fenley).
- One was killed by a fall from a ship's masthead.

Some of the entries come directly from Portland's vital records, but they often summarize a cause of death in one or two words. When the entry is unusual, it leaves us wanting to know more; that's when I get to work! I've spent a great deal of time searching for the backstories of people buried at Eastern Cemetery. The trigger is sometimes the burial record, but just as often it's an interesting gravestone. It's also important to note that countless other people lost their lives similarly to those documented in these burial records, but their own burial records are silent on their causes of death.

JOHN SHEAFE (1809–1838)

Jordan's record for John Sheafe reads, "Son of William and Mary, died 7 September 1838 at age twenty-nine years. Lost from the brig *Alna*, on the Florida coast." His vital record gives his name, age, burial location and incorrectly lists his father's name as John (it's William). I found his name on the nicely carved slate marker memorializing his mother, Mary. She died in 1831, seven years before her son, but the gravestone there today was placed after John passed.

I was in Florida at the time I was working on this chapter, so my interest was piqued by the fact that John Sheafe had died there. Fortunately, the events that brought about his death were documented in books published by Charles Ellms in 1841 and George Buker in 1975, along with some naval journals of the day.

The story of John Sheafe and the other men aboard the *Alna* was best told by two Portland sailors who survived the ordeal: Eleazer Wyer Jr. and Samuel Cammett. Five of the seven aboard were Portland-based,

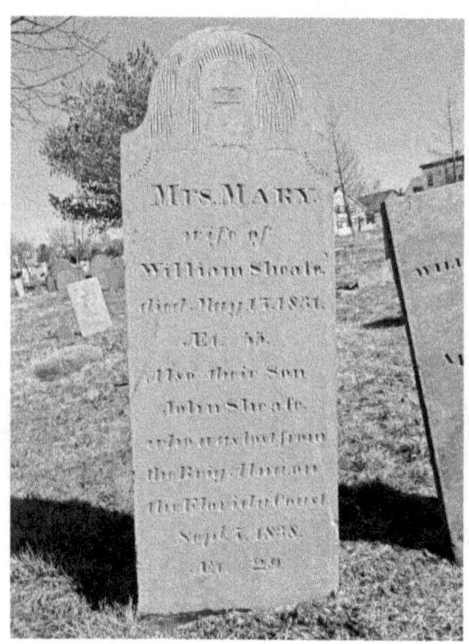

The marker for Mary Sheafe and her son John, who was lost at sea in 1838.

including Captain Charles Thomas (born in 1801), first mate Andrew J. Plummer and seaman John Sheafe. The cook, William Reed, was from Salem, Massachusetts, and the last crew member was a Dutchman named Ryan. The *Alna* was a seventy-three-foot, 118-ton schooner built in Alna, Maine, in 1835.

The *Alna* left Cuba on August 18, 1838, for the journey north. But the winds were too light for Captain Thomas to make any headway. When the winds finally picked up on September 5, they came on far too strong from the northeast, which did not help the captain in his efforts to sail the ship to New England. The *Alna* was about fifteen miles off the south Florida coast, and over the course of two days, the winds reached gale force, continuously pushing the ship toward land. The captain realized that he would lose control and that the ship would sink or be wrecked by crashing ashore. Knowing it was impossible to remain at sea, he decided to run the ship directly toward the beach, with the hopes of saving his crew from sure death and minimizing damage to the vessel and cargo. The wind-blown waves were so large they were washing completely over the deck, carrying everything loose over the side. As one huge wave swept over the ship on September 7, it took John Sheafe with it.

The Florida Beach

Despite the loss of his crewman, the captain was successful in his plan to beach the boat that day, and the *Alna* hit sand. The waves had pushed it close enough to the beach so that the men could jump directly from ship to shore. Landfall was about twenty miles north of Cape Florida (or about halfway between today's cities of Miami and Fort Lauderdale). When the winds and the sea finally calmed, the six men recovered as much food, water and other provisions from the ship as they could, reportedly enough to keep them alive a month. With patrol boats occasionally running along

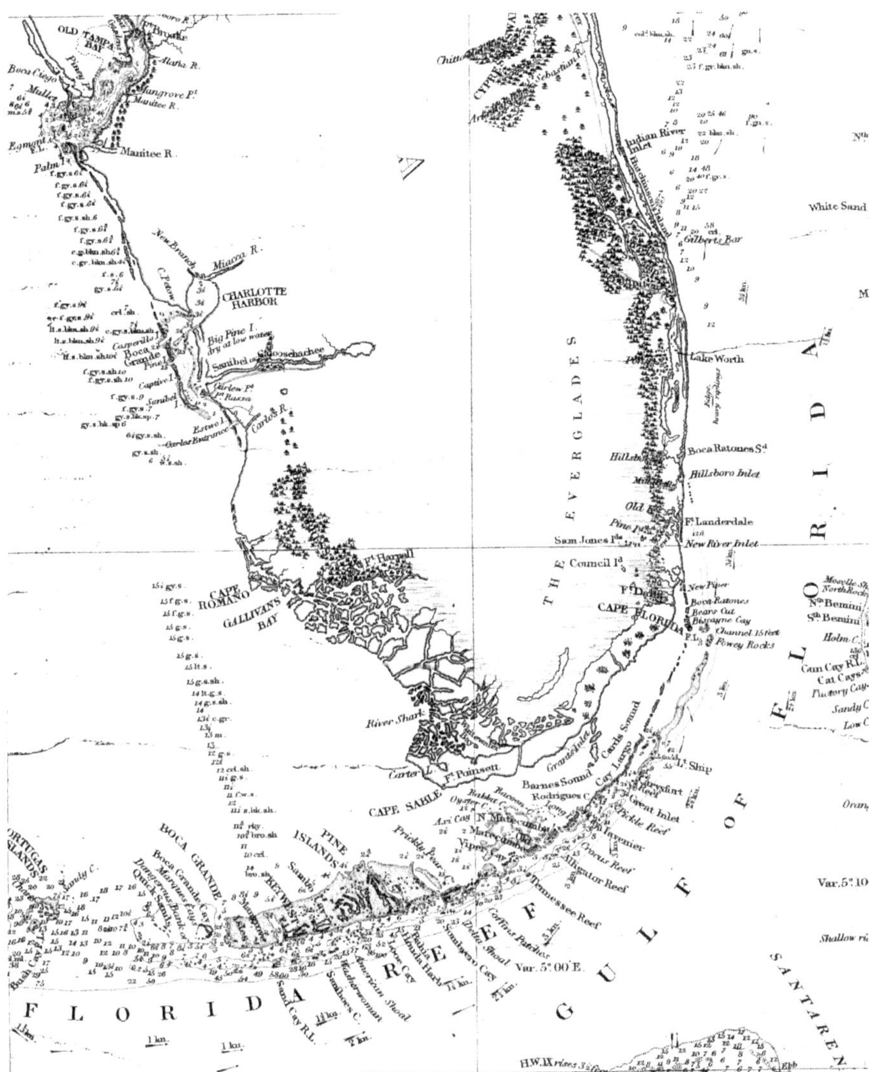

Detail of an 1848 Florida map showing the coastline where the *Alna* was beached in 1838. The landing site was on the east coast halfway between Fort Lauderdale and Cape Florida. *Courtesy of NOAA's Office of Coast Survey Historical Map & Chart Collection.*

Florida's coast and trade ships regularly running between the Caribbean and New England, they expected to be rescued soon.

Sheafe's body was never recovered. The events that followed his death were recorded by Wyer in a letter he wrote from aboard his rescue ship, from later interviews conducted with Wyer and Cammett and from the journal of the lieutenant commander of their rescue ship. The following is compiled from those accounts.

On the morning of Sunday, September 9, Cammett returned to the ship to retrieve the captain's spyglass, to be used for making a fire. The captain and Cammett went on a five-mile scouting walk south but found nothing. Wyer wrote, "About noon, the first Indians which appeared [near] our tent were four in number. They were armed with rifles. The mate was packing his clothes in his chest, which he had been drying that day; and the first notice we had of the Indians was the smart crack of a rifle; and at the same instant the mate exclaimed 'O dear!' having received the ball in his hand, passing into the abdomen."

Despite his injury, first mate Plummer started to run barefoot down the beach, along with Ryan and the cook. Wyer went into the tent to tell the captain and Cammett that the Indians were attacking, but the captain told them that the Indians would not harm them unless they tried to run. Wyer wrote, "The same Indian, being behind a tree, released and marked me for his next object, which gave me the ball through the hand, passing up

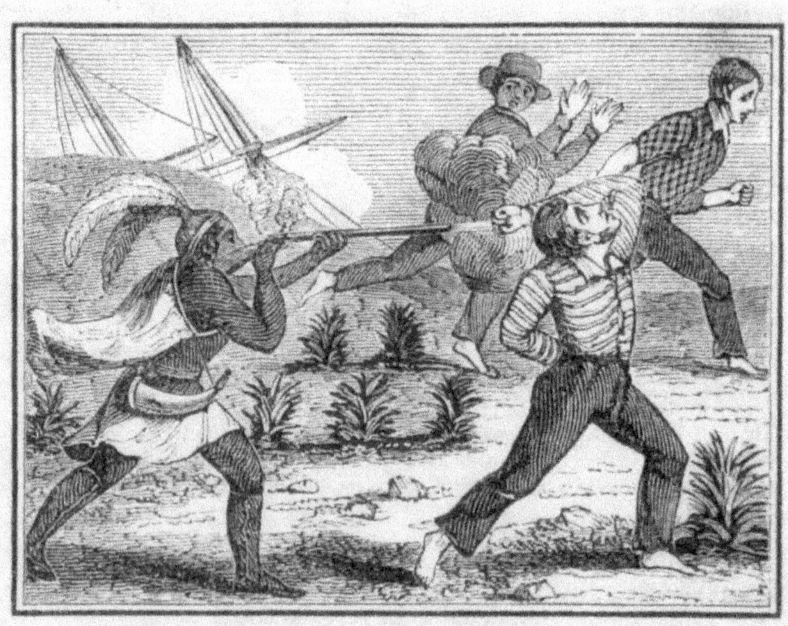

The Indian attack on the Florida beach. *From* The Tragedy of the Seas, *Charles Ellms, 1841.*

laterally through the thigh, coming out just below the hip joint, making a journey through the flesh of eight or nine inches." The three of them then also began to run up the beach, with the Indians in pursuit. Wyer noted that the captain's earlier walk had left him exhausted, so he "could not keep up with us, and being behind, the Indians overtook him. We halted, being thirty yards ahead of him, to see what his fate might be. Upon his knees he begged for his life, but…I saw him shot, and he fell on his face and seemed to die instantly."

Sheafe and Captain Thomas were now dead, and Plummer, critically wounded, was soon to follow. Buker wrote that the Indians captured the cook and Ryan and forced them to work around their camp for the remainder of the day. "At dusk they were taken out to be shot. The cook was killed immediately, but Ryan, although shot at, managed to escape in the darkness." Ryan returned to the *Alna* and stayed hidden below deck that night and the following day. Once it was clear to him that the Indians were nowhere nearby, he emerged and was able to flag down a passing ship to his rescue.

Wyer and Cammett Are Separated

Wyer's account continued:

> *I felt approaching weakness from loss of blood, and I feared I must soon give up. We very soon entered the bushes, Cammett going ahead. I soon lost him, and made my way along until night among the palmettos which cut my feet cruelly; added to this were mosquitoes, which were a formidable foe. At dark, on Sunday night, I came out on the beach and travelled till nearly daylight. Finding my wounds bleeding profusely, I tore off the bottom of my flannel shirt, and bound them up….They continued to bleed all the next day. I lay down, and sometimes fell down, often thinking I should not be able to rise again.*

Cammett explained that when he and Wyer got separated in the bushes on Sunday,

> *I remained quiet, in concealment, until the dusk of the evening; then I thought it prudent to start. I walked…along the beach five or six miles and encountered a party of Indians. They saw me, and raised a horrid yell,*

> *and pursued me. I ran into a swamp, where the mud and water were about waist high. Two Indians remained where I entered, while the rest seemed to be surrounding me; they avoided the water on account of the snakes. I was about an hour there—concluded it would not do to stop until morning, for they would get me—got out, and took to the shore…was careful to go so close to the shore that every ripple of water should wash out my tracks.*

He finally reached a river and waded in up to his neck, traversed it and noted that he "began to feel as if I was delivered."

On Monday, Wyer reported that he continued to travel the beach, eventually finding a large river that he struggled to cross. "Here I was about to despair. I finally got foothold and gained the shore, but found myself very much exhausted. I should think the river was a quarter mile wide. It was about night. I kept on—occasionally would lie down during the night gathering sea-weed to cover me while asleep—when I awoke, would go on again till weary, then take a nap." In the meantime, Cammett's account of Monday included that he was still on the river and that the growth of trees and bushes along the edge required him to swim instead of walk. He found an island in the middle of the river and swam to it, noting "the roots of the trees starting out two or three feet above ground, making a sort of bridge to walk on—tasted the water and found it fresh—stopped and rested—a severe current on both sides. Seeing a number of sharks, I made a raft of driftwood; but it was waterlogged and would not support me." Eventually, Cammett did reach the beach again and continued to walk. "My feet were deeply cut with shells and palmettos, and ankles so swollen, I could not bend them—my toes raw up between, and cruelly sore."

On Tuesday and Wednesday, both men, on separate paths, continued to walk the beach and cross streams, wary of Indians and hoping to find a passing ship to rescue them. Both reported eating dead fish they found washed on the beach. Wyer said, "A dead fish was a great luxury; and when I had sated my appetite, I would put them on my hat to dry, while journeying onward." He noted that while the dead fish were plentiful, so were the "acres of pelicans" that ate them—so many, in fact, that the fish were all consumed before they could rot. Wyer reported needing to cross a river with alligators lining its banks and "full of sharks of the largest kind." He wrote, "I was divested of fear, and I plunged in and landed safely on the other side, feeling no enemy to be worse than the Indians." Cammett suffered from the intense heat, noting that he "had no hat and was obliged to wet my head to keep it cool." He found a wrecked ship on the beach and slept on it Tuesday, "my neck so swollen with mosquito bites that I could scarcely move my head." On Wednesday, he crawled into a large hollow log to nap but was stung by a centipede. Wyer, in the meantime, was trying to rest while up a tree, but a snake "his size round was as large as my ankle" was already there.

Rescued, at Last

It was a good thing that Cammett was bitten by the centipede, for as he woke up to the sting, he noticed four sloops traveling offshore. He hoisted a tar bucket he'd found up on a pole and began waving it, but none of the passing ships saw him right away, and he reported getting no sleep on the beach that night. But the next day, Thursday, the men aboard the ship *Mount Vernon* did see him and sent a boat ashore to rescue him. As the rowboat neared the ship, Cammett heard the voice of his friend Wyer calling his name. Wyer had been rescued Wednesday evening. He'd tied his shirt on a pole and waved it with all his strength and, being seen by the men on the *Mount Vernon*, was taken aboard, a rescued man. From the *Mount Vernon*, the men transferred to two other boats before making their way back home.

In the report filed by the lieutenant commander of the schooner *Wave*, we learn that the storm had wrecked a half dozen ships along the south Florida coast; some crews had been completely lost at sea, other survivors had been attended to by the Seminoles (if French) or killed by them (if American). The *Wave* came to the rescue of at least one other ship the day it found the *Alna*. The report read, "Found the wreck of the brig *Alna*, Capt. Thomas of Portland, Maine, on the eastern coast, about twenty-five miles north of Cape Florida, in the possession of a small party of Indians. Her crew had been murdered, with the exception of two. We killed three and wounded two of the Indians in their flight, and destroyed three canoes. Found the bodies of two of the brig's crew and burnt [the ship]."

A review of vital records for Wyer and Cammett suggests both men returned to Portland to live out their lives. Captain Thomas is memorialized on a marker at Portland's Evergreen Cemetery; John Sheafe's is found at Eastern Cemetery at plot C-94.

Chapter 12

THREE BANK ROBBERS

On April 16, 1850, William Thomas entered Eastern Cemetery, seeking a private spot under a tree, behind a large monument or otherwise hidden away from the eyes of the town's passersby. Then, he drank to excess. He was found dead in the cemetery the next day, and his vital record indicates his cause of death was "intemperance."

Those of us who serve as tour guides for Spirits Alive always look for interesting stories to share with our visitors. Many include Daniel Manley on our walks; his burial record alone suggests a good story, noting him as "Portland's first bank robber." The incident that brought Daniel Manley's name to infamy occurred in 1818. But Manley really wasn't the first; I stumbled across this passage in the *Chronicles of Casco Bay*, published in 1850: "January 12, 1807: The Maine Bank was broken into Saturday evening and robbed of about two thousand dollars. An Irishman was apprehended and a part of the money discovered under a barn, concealed in an old pair of pantaloons." The Irishman's identity remains unknown, so we don't know if he later died in Portland and ended up in Eastern Cemetery's Catholic Ground.

The Banks

The Maine Bank opened in 1802, the second established in Portland. It had been operating for only five years at the time of the Irishman's robbery. The first bank in town was the Portland Bank, which had opened in 1800. The preferred currency during this period was the silver dollar, although a few Boston-based banks were issuing paper currency. Portland had a robust maritime trade economy, and a group of Portland business owners decided that it was time for the town to have its own bank and the ability to produce paper currency. Among the organizers of the first bank was John Taber, a Quaker whom we met in chapter 8. And so with approval by the court, the Portland Bank opened with starting capital of $100,000 (very roughly converted to today's dollars, about $2 million). The Portland Bank—like so many businesses—failed during the trade embargo years and suspended operations by 1810. The Cumberland Bank next emerged, incorporating in 1812 as Portland's third bank.

Daniel Manley (1774-1837)

When I first heard the story of Daniel Manley, I recall it ending with the discovery of the stolen cash by clam diggers in the mudflats of Scarborough Marsh, just south of Portland. That may have been added over time as a crowd-pleasing embellishment. The true story, as found in a series of newspaper articles at the time, is really quite interesting on its own.

On Sunday, August 2, 1818, Joseph Swift, the cashier at the Cumberland Bank, had reason to go to the bank and found the doors unlocked. He also discovered that over $200,000 was missing from the vault—a huge sum for the time. He immediately reported the theft to the bank's directors and documented the specific losses in an inventory that was published as a reward notice. That notice was dated August 2, signed by Swift and entitled "High-handed Robbery!" The fact that the bank had been completely cleaned out was indeed big news, and there was said to be a great deal of excitement and concern in town.

In that first notice, the bank offered $500 to "whoever will detect and bring to conviction the thief or thieves" and up to $1,000 for the return of the entire amount of the property stolen (with partial proportionate reward paid if the recovery was less than the total stolen). Missing from the bank was about $195,000 in Cumberland Bank bills, about $1,000 each in old Portland Bank and Maine Bank bills, a $500 note from the Boston-based Mechanics and Manufacturer's Bank, $1,600 in gold specie (coins) and $5,400 in silver specie. The notice also described the majority of the Cumberland Bank bills being of larger denominations—fifties, twenties and tens—most of which had not been put into circulation. The bank cautioned, "All good citizens are earnestly called upon not to receive any such bills, because, having been stolen, they will not be paid by the Bank."

There was no organized police force yet in Portland. Instead, a loosely organized group of night watchmen could be found patrolling the town. So the investigation of this crime was handled by the inspector of the night watch, though some of the bank directors aided in his investigation. A small amount of the loot was found on Sunday night in the yard behind the bank, leading the investigator to believe that the thieves had been alarmed by someone in the neighborhood and, in their haste to flee out the back entrance, dropped some of the cash. His hope was that more of the stolen money would be discovered in the yard at daybreak, but no more was found that Monday morning.

On Tuesday, August 4, a broadside was printed notifying the public that the reward money had been boosted to $10,000. The *Eastern Argus* newspaper reported, "Several persons have been apprehended on suspicion." One of those was the blacksmith, Mr. Ellis. The team had quickly realized that no locks were broken at the bank and suspected that a false key may have been forged. Ellis was found to be innocent and released, but he offered some information that led the investigators to Daniel Manley, who was apprehended and held in custody for questioning. The paper reported, "The investigation was continued all day Tuesday, and several circumstances were brought to light that greatly enhanced the suspicions against Manley." The paper did not provide details, but they are found in the accounting of the incident by William E. Gould in his address to the Maine Historical Society in 1883:

> *The doors and locks were not of present construction. The directors had sent their locks over to Ellis, the blacksmith, to be fixed up; common blacksmith work was all that was then necessary. While they were in his shop, they were inspected by one Daniel Manley, who had been keeping a sort of junk store near Clay Cove and who had removed to near the head of Long Wharf. Manley was a shrewd fellow, and as he saw the locks and keys of the bank lying around Ellis' shop, he conceived the idea of taking an impression*

10,000 DOLLARS

REWARD.

ON Saturday night last, the *Cumberland Bank* was entered by false keys, and robbed of over

TWO HUNDRED THOUSAND DOLLARS.

About *one hundred ninety-five thousand dollars* in bills of that Bank, and about *nine thousand dollars* in bills of other Banks—About *sixteen hundred dollars* in Gold, and *five thousand four hundred dollars* in Silver. A part of the specie has been recovered.

The Cumberland Bank bills taken, were Fifties, Twenties and Tens. There are no fifties nor twenty dollar bills, and very few ten dollar bills, lawfully in circulation. This circumstance may lead to detection. And all good citizens are cautioned not to receive such bills, because, having been stolen, they will not be paid at the Bank. Among the bills of other Banks, were perhaps *one thousand dollars* of the old Portland Bank, and about *one thousand dollars* of Maine Bank bills. There was also a *five hundred dollar* note on the *Mechanic and Manufacturers Bank* in Boston.

Whoever will procure the whole of the money so lost to be restored to the Bank, shall receive ***NINE THOUSAND DOLLARS*** in addition to the sum already offered in their advertisement of the 2d current, and in that proportion for whatever sum may be recovered and restored to the Bank.

By order of the Directors of the Cumberland Bank.

Portland, August 4, 1818. ***JOSEPH SWIFT***, Cashier.

A broadside announcing the reward for the return of money stolen from the Cumberland Bank in 1818. *Collections of Maine Historical Society (www.MaineMemory.net, Item #20128).*

of the keys for the time of need. He goes to Joseph Noble's foundry and borrows some molding sand to get the form of the keys. Manley evidently succeeded well in getting the impression of the keys.

Captain Benjamin Rolfe (1780–1818)

By Wednesday, the investigators were zeroing in on Manley, but they also apprehended Manley's associate Captain Benjamin Rolfe for questioning. Captain Rolfe was a first-generation colonial, born in Portland in 1780 to parents who had emigrated from France. He married Rebecca Williams in 1804 and had seven children with her before she died in 1816. Five months later, he married Nancy Bangs, who bore him one more child. Though he was a sea captain, he owned a large farm in Gorham, Maine, and lived there from 1813 to 1818. Soon after moving to Portland, he became tangled up with Manley.

The inspector offered the captain a reward in exchange for his full disclosure of involvement, and Rolfe took the deal. He told the inspector that the robbery had been planned for a while, that he and Manley were in it together—but no others—and that the duo had entered the bank during some practice runs a few nights prior to the actual robbery. He clearly implicated Manley as mastermind, claiming that he had been reluctantly drawn into the scheme by his "unprincipled and audacious associate."

Rolfe returned $1,600 that he had first concealed from the inspector and told the inspector and his associates that he'd bring them to the waterfront location where Manley had decided to hide the money. On Thursday, they went to the spot, but the cash was not found. He'd been double-crossed by Manley! According to the newspaper report, "Thursday morning, when Rolfe was endeavoring, without success, to find the remainder of the specie, he withdrew from custody for a few minutes into a deep ravine, and closed his unhappy career with a small pocket pistol that he carried about him concealed. The report was so slight that it was not heard by those who stood but a few paces from him. Thinking that his absence was longer than necessary, his keepers followed his steps, and found him stretched on the ground a lifeless corpse."

Eastern Cemetery has an 1843 burial record for Rolfe's infant grandson Benjamin (the fourth generation so named). While there is no record of the captain's burial at Eastern Cemetery, certainly he is there, since he was at the time a resident of Portland and killed himself along the waterfront just steps from the town's only cemetery.

To Scarborough Marsh, Then to Jail

The bank's canvas coin bag was found in Manley's garden. The investigators knew they had their man. They told him that Rolfe had made a complete confession and suggested that to save himself, he admit guilt. He did. But the money was still missing, so the investigators proposed a deal: they would give him the posted reward if he led them to the cash. Manley agreed, and they recovered a small amount he'd buried in his garden. He then brought them to Scarborough. The search for the exact spot attracted a few neighbors to the site, and it was actually the neighbors who discovered the loot. They claimed the reward that had been promised to Manley, and it was ultimately split evenly between them. How interesting that Manley was actually able to

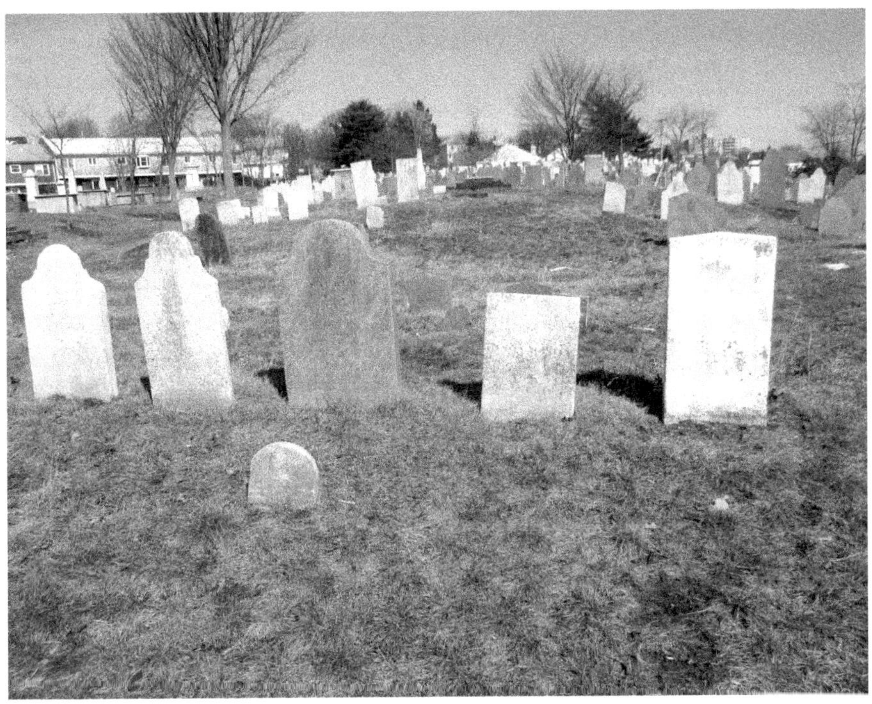

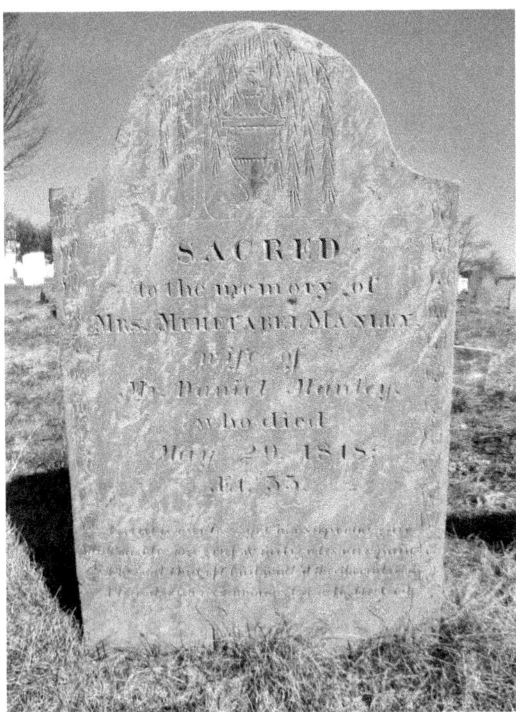

Above: The family lot for Daniel Manley. His marker is the short, square-topped white marble, second from the right. It is heavily eroded and illegible.

Left: The marker for Mehitable Manley. Abel Davis misspelled her name as Mehetabel but carved a beautiful bellflower border on her slate.

benefit financially for his crime—not an outcome we'd expect for a modern-day robbery. But Manley paid his price. On Friday, just under a week after the robbery, he went back to jail to await his trial before the Supreme Court.

On September 5, Manley's brother-in-law Fobes Dela was also sent to jail for providing Manley with supplies he might use to break out of prison. He was a grocer in town, married and the father of a half dozen children. According to the *Eastern Argus*, Dela had furnished Manley with "a knife, a pistol, powder and ball, a vial of aquafortis, a tinder-box, tinder, steel, flint, matches, and candles, which on search were found in the possession of Manley in a portable desk he had in his room."

Once convicted, Manley spent the next twelve years in a Charlestown, Massachusetts jail. All of the stolen cash, but for one small bag of gold, had been returned to the bank. Manley returned to Portland after his incarceration. His wife had passed, but a son and daughter were still alive in 1830, by now young adults. He lived his final seven years as a free man and died in 1837 at the age of sixty-three of unknown causes. The marble marker on his grave is illegible due to weathering of the stone, but it is said to have been carved with the words "Portland's first bank robber."

Daniel Manley's gravestone is located in a family lot in Section E, at grave 47. To one side is his unmarried daughter Emily (Emeline), who died in 1887 in her seventies. Her marble marker is also quite eroded and difficult to read. On the other side is Mehitable (Dailey) Manley, his wife, whose name appears as "Hitty" in some vital records. She died just before the bank robbery in 1818 at age thirty-five. Her slate marker was carved by Abel Davis, one of the men who worked in the Adams shop in the 1820s. Davis misspelled her name as "Mehetabel." Others in the lot are daughter Catherine, who died in 1813 at age six, and some in-laws from the Dela family.

Chapter 13

HOW MANY ARE BURIED?

One of the last burials at Eastern Cemetery was for Laura S. Cross Pittee, entombed in 1896. Laura was born in 1843 to Francis and Cornelia Cross. Francis was a stair builder; Cornelia raised at least five children. Laura married a carpenter—Charles T. Pittee—in Portland in 1875, and their daughter, Mabel Alice, arrived soon after. Laura lost Charles in 1888 to an accident (he was forty-eight) and Mabel Alice to consumption in 1889 (she was thirteen). Drifting from one address to another in the following five years, Laura ended up in Augusta, Maine, where she died—"insane"—on December 3, 1896.

We will never know the exact number of people who are at rest in Eastern Cemetery. Sources vary greatly in their estimates of the number interred. In an effort to zero in on a more exact number, I conducted two exercises: I analyzed samples of population and mortality data for Portland during the years that the cemetery was the sole burying ground on the peninsula, and I manually repopulated the cemetery (on paper!) using Goodwin's 1890 plot map. In October 2015, I published the results in a paper that is available at the Maine Historical Society in its collections on Eastern Cemetery.

Sources for burial numbers include:

- 2,744 mapped plots (Jordan's 1987 revision to the 1890 Goodwin survey map)
- 3,848 "named graves" (Commemorative Boulder off Funeral Lane, 1975)

- 3,920 interments (*Record of Interments*, Bill Jordan, 1978)
- 4,136 "gravestones, monuments, grave sites" (Goodwin's survey of 1890)
- 6,738 interments (*Portland Cemetery Records* database)
- 6,829 interments (Find-A-Grave website for Eastern Cemetery)
- 7,000 "about 7,000 records" (Bill Jordan's 1987 *Burial Records...*)

Historian William Goold made a bold statement in this regard in 1886, when he wrote that Eastern Cemetery "was the principal place of burial belonging to the town until 1829, when it was estimated that the dead outnumbered the living within the corporate limits." This seems to have been an overstatement, as the population of Portland in 1830 exceeded twelve thousand.

I recognize the list above has an "apples to oranges" comparison problem. Other factors complicating the analysis include:

- Under-marked and unmarked graves. During the decades of settlement, lack of easy access to carved gravestones meant that the dead were simply put in graves marked with a piece of field stone or wood (under-marked), if at all (unmarked). Mass graves may have been used during severe disease outbreaks. As well, Quakers, African Americans and strangers were often buried in unmarked graves for religious or economic reasons.
- Cenotaphs. Memorials for those who are buried elsewhere are common. Eastern Cemetery has a good number of cenotaphs, so the marker appears on the map and is counted on the plot survey, but the person is not actually within the burial ground.
- Lack of record-keeping. For its first 150 years, the Burying Ground received the dead without record of who they were or where they were buried. The journals of the Reverends Smith and Deane contain countless names of people who died in Portland in the 1700s for whom no burial listing is found in Jordan's list of interments.
- Mass exodus. The three new cemeteries (Western, Evergreen and Calvary) established in the 1800s took the pressure off the problem of overcrowding at Eastern. As families purchased larger plots in these burial grounds, it was common practice to remove remains from Eastern for reburial in new plots. Today, this creates a challenge in the effort to find Eastern Cemetery's

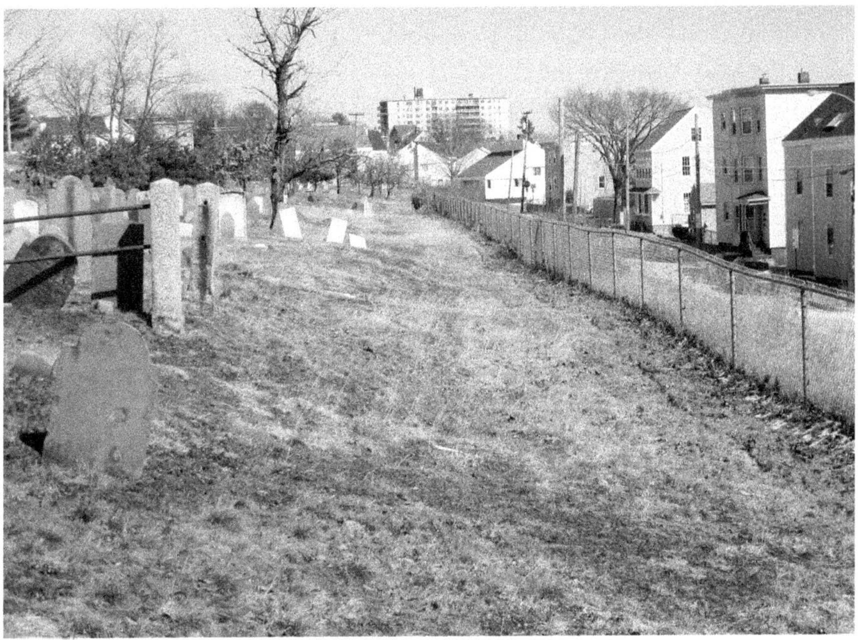

The fifteen-foot-wide space that today runs the entire length of the southern border of the cemetery, created when the retaining wall was constructed after the 1866 fire.

total number of burials, as some records may not accurately reflect where these people actually rest.

- Loss of historic burial land. As discussed in chapter 4, land (containing human remains?) on the southern edge was lost in the post-fire reconstruction. Today, there is a fifteen-foot-wide vacant space that runs the entire length of the cemetery's back fence. It appears that when the city extended Federal Street and built the retaining wall, workers back-filled this area (to create a walkway?). This open space seems far too orderly in its lack of grave markers, given all of the early graves immediately adjoining it.
- Strangers' Grounds. Chapter 9 provides more detail about these, and we know that the city allowed two bodies per grave in those patches. While not contributing greatly to the overall total interred, this does reflect our inability to find an exact number.
- Loss of markers. Whether by vandalism, theft, accidental damage or natural deterioration, there has been a significant loss of grave markers over the years.

- Reuse of graves. Goold, Jordan and other sources suggest that the old section of the cemetery had plots that were used more than once. It's hard to nail this down, but if true, it does affect the total number interred.

ANALYSIS OF POPULATION AND MORTALITY

My first attempt to find the number of people interred was to simply add up the number of people known to have died each year in Portland. However, annual mortality figures are not available for much of the first 150 years of the cemetery's history, and a simple summing of all the deceased isn't possible. By the early 1800s, annual reports were more reliably published.

I decided to use population and mortality data to assign an average value of "deaths per 1,000" and then apply it to the known population through about 1800, when mortality numbers became more available. I selected the 1770s decade, since values for both population and mortality were found in Willis, Elwell and the *Portland City Guide*. The results were:

Year	Deaths per 1,000
1772	18
1773	37
1774	20
1776	7
1778	4

It seemed odd that the death rate was ten times greater in 1773 than in 1778, and I began to suspect some inconsistencies in reporting. For example, population statistics were reported for Portland Neck, but death and burial statistics may have sometimes extended beyond the Neck to Stroudwater Cemetery, which was active by then. Other factors may include particularly challenging disease cycles, resulting in a higher death rate than usual. Extracting an average deaths per one thousand value seemed unreliable, at best, and after some thought, I decided that this was proving to be of little help.

Repopulating the Cemetery

My second exercise was a relatively simple, yet time-consuming, task. Starting with the assumption that unmarked plots are in fact occupied, I repopulated the open areas of the cemetery section by section, line by line. This worked well for the open areas. One known problem was that some families set aside family lots consisting of six or eight graves, not all of which ended up being occupied. Another was that in the field of tombs in Section A there is an assumption that 30 people could be buried per tomb, for a total capacity there of 2,550, yet not all tombs were filled to capacity. According to the *Record of Interments*, tombs with the greatest number of burials were Tomb A-69 with 28 people, A-29 with 26 and A-72 with 24.

Had this field of tombs been laid out as the rest of the burial ground (that is, one person per plot), total capacity of the area would have been

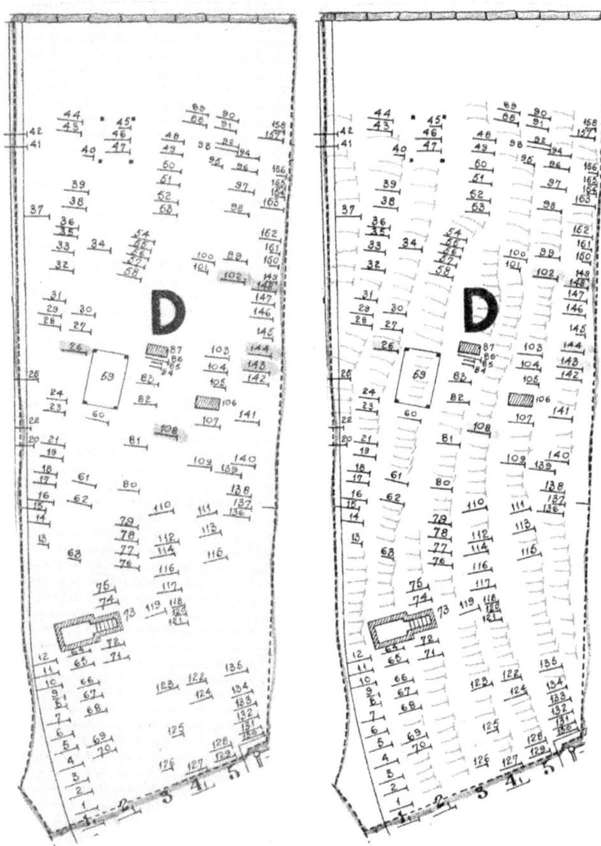

A before and after comparison of Section D, used to calculate total capacity of the cemetery by the author. The before image is from the 1890 map showing 158 known graves; the after image shows that this section has the capacity of at least 350 graves.

approximately six hundred. So the tombs allowed many more interments than if this area had been left an open burial field.

As stated at the outset, it's impossible to know the exact number of people buried at Eastern Cemetery. Many variables are at play and move the estimate higher or lower. But I was able to find an approximate *capacity* of 6,250 graves. If we are to believe that some graves in the original burial ground were used more than once or that remains were removed when the hillside was carved away at Federal Street, then this capacity increases. But by how much—10 percent? The fact that many bodies were removed to other burial grounds brings the number of burials back down. Again, by how much?

The purpose of this was to consider a variety of variables and find a more reliable number of interments within the currently used range of four thousand to seven thousand. All things considered, I certainly confirmed the challenge of ever finding a good number, but I determined that a reasonable *estimate* of the number of people who were (once or forever) buried at Eastern Cemetery is about seven thousand.

Chapter 14

WHERE ARE THEY BURIED?

John H. Burbank, age sixteen, was buried in two pieces in 1860. Ten years earlier, his family was farming in Augusta, Maine, but then relocated to Boston. There, John's only sister, Laurietta (age eighteen), died of smallpox in 1856, and there his father died in 1857. John and his mother, Ann, then moved to Portland. On October 24, 1860, John died of consumption and was buried in an unmarked spot located at the foot of Thomas Bolton's grave (plot H-124). His burial note reads, "His arm was interred in June."

The roster that provides the basis for our knowledge about who lies where came from the work of City Engineer William Goodwin in 1890. Though it's good that we have those records, it is important to keep in mind that the cemetery was already well over two hundred years old, had been closed to new burials for fifty years, had lost its original southern slope and had been for decades vandalized, neglected and subjected to natural deterioration. In an effort to organize the records, Goodwin divided the cemetery into sections and assigned plot numbers. With so many graves being unmarked or with grave markers destroyed, it's no surprise that many of the burial record notes are no longer helpful.

There are 350 people whose burial records provide a location description but no specific plot numbers. Many indicate "GSL," meaning that the gravestone has been lost; others are silent on this, so the assumption is the grave was never marked. Most common are those such as the one for Abner Bagley (died 1843), which reads, "Buried by side of Green's stone." There are eleven people named Green who were buried prior to Abner's death, making it impossible to find a location. In other cases, the record can lead us to a specific spot. For example, Lizzie Leighton died in 1859, and her note reads, "Buried near DeSanchez." While she has no grave marker on her plot, we know that she is near the one person named DeSanchez, who is at plot B-12-1.

The three most common notes are, "Buried at the head of ——," "Buried at the foot of ——" and "Buried at the side of ——" (someone else's) grave. These locator notes work fine when the someone else is known. But far too often this is not the case. One example of a helpful note is for Ellen Ann Lenham, who died in 1846 and was buried "at the foot of Lucy Moody's grave." We can pinpoint her exact location as being at the foot of plot G-21 (which is, in fact, the one and only Lucy Moody interred).

Other indicators may have been useful for a short time, such as the record for John Kelly (died 1848), which reads, "Buried at the foot of Mary Barbour's grave," or the note for an infant child named Mahan (died 1856), which reads, "Buried beside Bolles' child's grave near corner." At the time of these burials, stones must have been in place for Mary Barbour and the Bolles child, but now their grave markers no longer exist, and we are led nowhere when trying to find these graves.

Some notes are quite specific in their attempt to hone us in. Two examples are for Mary Stevens (died 1854), who was "Buried three paces west of Jacob Noyes' stone," and John Anderson (died 1854), who was "Buried four feet east of Mother Finney's stone." My favorite among these is the note for Enoch Freeman, Portland's first register of deeds (died 1788). With no paper records being kept at the time, he decided to give directions to the graves of his four children by having them carved onto his own gravestone, noting they were "S 17 degrees W, four or five rods from this grave." While in the day one would have needed a compass and knowledge of the length of a rod, today we simply check the *Record of Interments* and plot maps. In fact, four grave markers are found for the children of Enoch and Mary Freeman. They predeceased their father and were buried in a cluster about seventy feet southwest of his grave.

Some burial notes place plots near structures that are no longer standing. Among these are George Bartlett (1846), "Buried near the Hearse House"; Alonzo Chickering (1846), "Buried at side of the fence near the corner of the Ladder House"; and Harrison Turner (1845), "Buried near the Tool House."

Still other notes are truly completely useless. Cynthia Clapp (1857) was "Buried on the low flat ground," Sarah Lunt was "Buried near the pathway,"

James Trumbull (1851) was "Buried on the side of the hill" and Alma Paine (1849) was "Buried near the turn of the road." Records such as these are common, and we will never know where the people are.

Notes are not limited to people who were buried in the open ground but can be found for those in tombs as well. Many records indicate people who were buried in someone else's tomb. Mary Eustis Adams (1853) was "Buried in David Dana's tomb." We know David Dana's tomb is A-74. In cross-checking the *Record of Interments*, we find that Tomb A-74 holds the remains of seven people named Dana but no Mary Adams. So how is it that she also ended up there?

One other example brings us to the next topic. The burial note for Julia Upham (1842) reads, "Buried John Mussey tomb." John Mussey's name does not appear in Jordan's book, but it does appear in the *Record of Interments*, with the note that he was moved. Mussey was a prominent banker and town leader. When his remains were moved from Tomb A-80 at Eastern Cemetery to Evergreen Cemetery, his family sold the tomb to Ezekiel Jordan. Nobody is listed on the Tomb A-80 roster in the *Record of Interments*, not even Julia Upham, which raises the question: did Julia Upham's remains also get moved out of the tomb? Or was a condition of the sale between the Musseys and Jordan that she would stay put? We'll probably never know.

Mass Exodus

People who were moved from Eastern Cemetery to other final resting places were sometimes transported with their original grave markers. There is a small collection of gravestones at Evergreen Cemetery that were carved in the shop of Bartlett Adams, who had died a generation before Evergreen even opened. Those ten stones memorialize people who died as early as 1805 and obviously were moved across town with their owners.

Some others left the original marker behind and put a new one in the new location, so that monuments in two locations now exist for them. An example is Martin O'Riley (died 1843), a Catholic whose grave at Eastern Cemetery has a marble stone. A second marker for him is found at Calvary Cemetery in South Portland.

Still others simply started over at the new cemetery with a new marker more in keeping with the style being produced at the time their loved one's remains were moved. John Mussey, mentioned just above, provides our

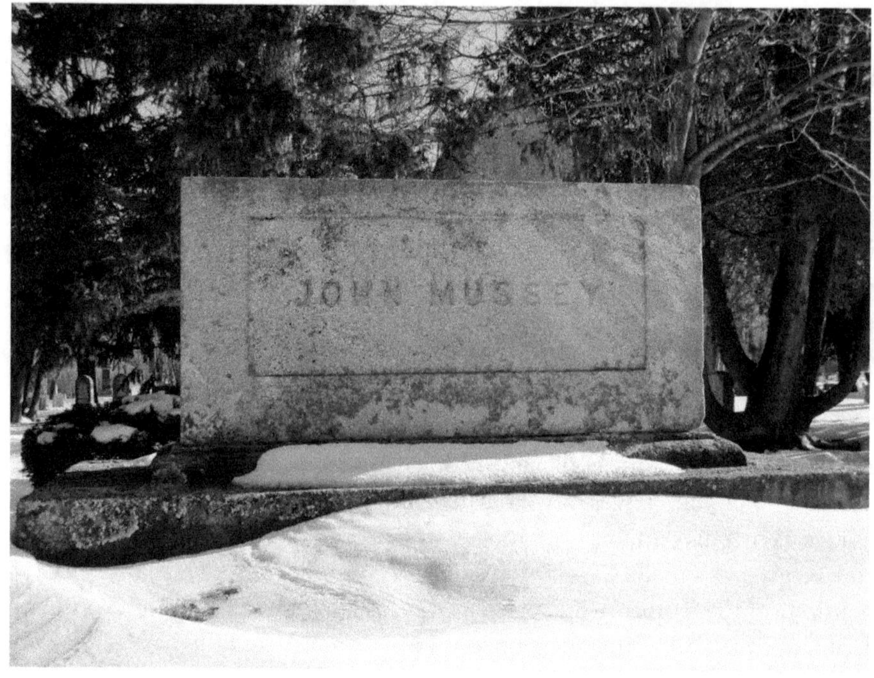

The front side of the monument for John Mussey at his new "final resting place," Evergreen Cemetery in Portland.

example. He died in 1817 and was first buried in Tomb A-80. Fifty-four years later, his remains were moved to Evergreen. His monument there is a large granite box tomb consistent with other midcentury markers in his new neighborhood.

We don't know the full extent of the exodus from Eastern Cemetery, but many prominent families apparently participated in this. The city actually encouraged it for a while, offering free lots at Evergreen Cemetery as long as families agreed to remove all bodies from their Eastern Cemetery lots. In 1868, reburial fees were set at $5.00 for the first adult body, $3.00 for each subsequent one and $3.50 for children. Goold lamented the removal of remains from the cemetery. He wrote, "A frequent excuse given for the removal of remains from Eastern Cemetery is, 'It is liable to have a street cut through it at any time,' but it should be recollected that this is the very way to hasten such a desecration; but the ground is not needed for that purpose." Further, "Under ordinary circumstances I think no one has any better right to remove the remains of a relative from their chosen place of burial, and

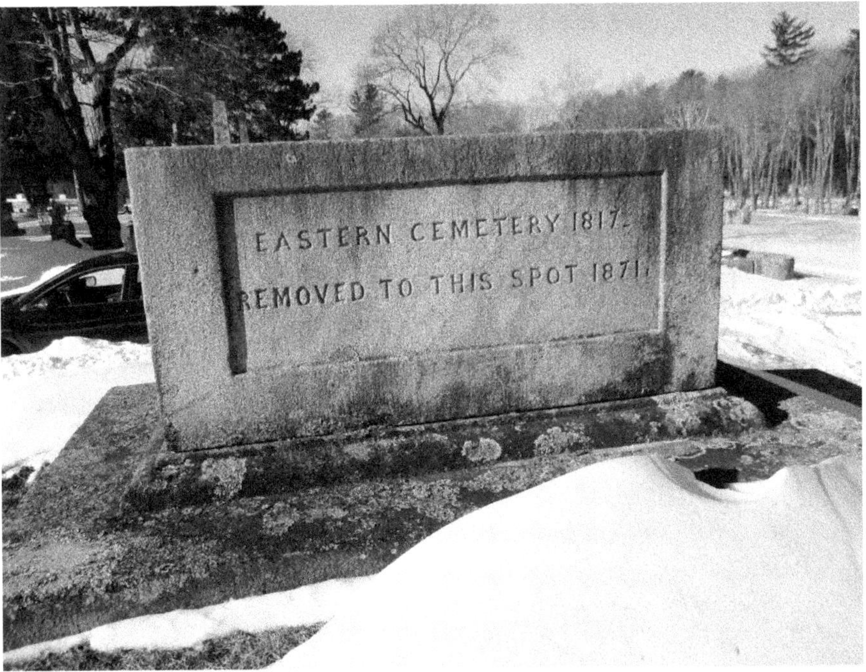

The back side of the Mussey monument showing that his original "final resting place" was Eastern Cemetery.

change the monument, than they have to disobey his attested will." He even got a bit otherworldly when saying, "I think it not unreasonable to suppose that the disembodied spirit, for a time at least, retains a knowledge of its former mortal tenement. This probability should be an incentive to us to surround our places of burial with all pleasant associations, and that they should be well cared for as a duty to the dead."

But removals were commonly done. Jordan's records include notes regarding transfer of remains for these well-known families: Baxter, Deering, Fessenden and Preble. Art Gaffar, historian at the Maine Charitable Mechanic Association, found record of the family of Henry Hill Boody doing the same. And recall from chapter 4 that when the underground tomb in Section A was entered to check for structural damage in 2010, remains of only two bodies were found, despite the fact that six people were listed as having been entombed there. The conclusion was made that four people had been moved out of the tomb and into another cemetery at some unknown time.

COMMODORE EDWARD PREBLE (1761–1807)

Commodore Edward Preble's remains were also moved from one tomb to another tomb at Eastern Cemetery. His funeral was well documented by Willam Goold and gives us some clues about early funeral ceremonies in Portland. Commodore Preble died in 1807 at the age of forty-six. His storied naval career included his command of "Old Ironsides" and battling pirates off Tripoli and led to a Congressional Medal and an 1806 invitation from President Thomas Jefferson to join his cabinet. Ill health prevented Preble from accepting that position, and he died of consumption within a year. Goold described the funeral, which began at the Preble house:

> *The coffin was then brought out, and the Masonic service was held in the front yard. All business of the town was suspended on the…day of the burial. Such a funeral pageant had never been seen in Portland. There was not a hearse in Cumberland County at that time. As was the custom, the coffin was carried on a bier on men's shoulders, covered with a black velvet pall, with cords and tassels at the side, held by the "pall bearers." On top of the pall was laid the Commodore's sword. There was not a carriage in the procession—all walked; even the bereaved wife was supported by her*

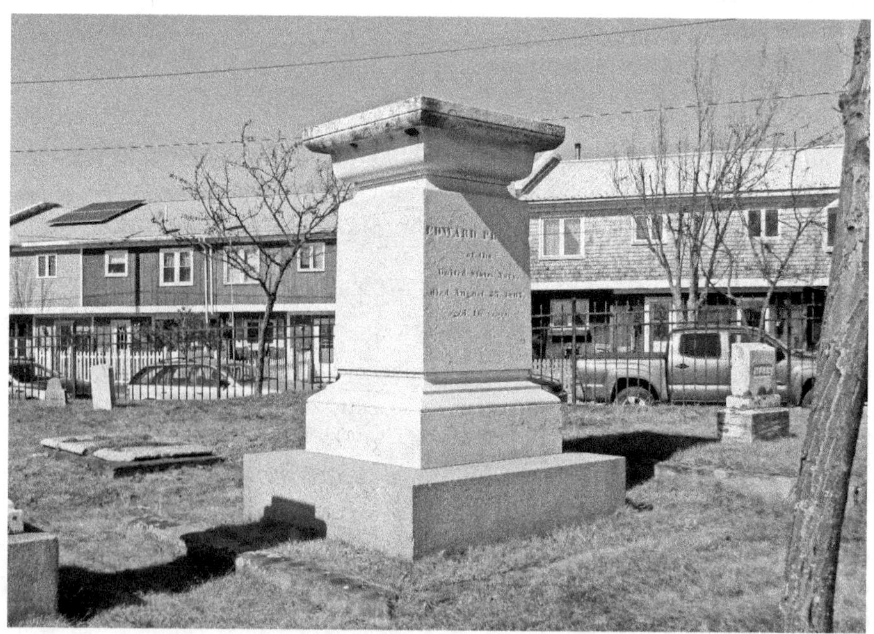

The monument for Commodore Edward Preble, found in Section A of the cemetery.

only brother, James Deering, and owing to the long route of the procession, her strength failed, and she left her place as chief mourner, and was assisted to a neighboring house. Commodore Preble's remains were first placed in the tomb of his father-in-law, Nathaniel Deering. At the time of the death of the Commodore's only child, Edward Deering Preble, in 1846, he had in process of building, a family tomb, in the same time-honored cemetery to which the remains of the father were removed.

Even Bartlett Adams's Children?

I've recently come to believe that Bartlett Adams moved three of his children from their original graves in Section I to his family tomb in Section A. In my first book, I noted they were buried in Section I, but something had always bugged me about the records for these three. In Jordan's book, Bartlett Jr., George and Eliza were listed as buried in plots I-201, I-202 and I-203. They died in 1806, 1809 and 1812, respectively. In the *Record of Interments*, their burial locations were listed both in Section I and the Adams-Rogers Tomb A-46. I believe Bartlett purchased the tomb around

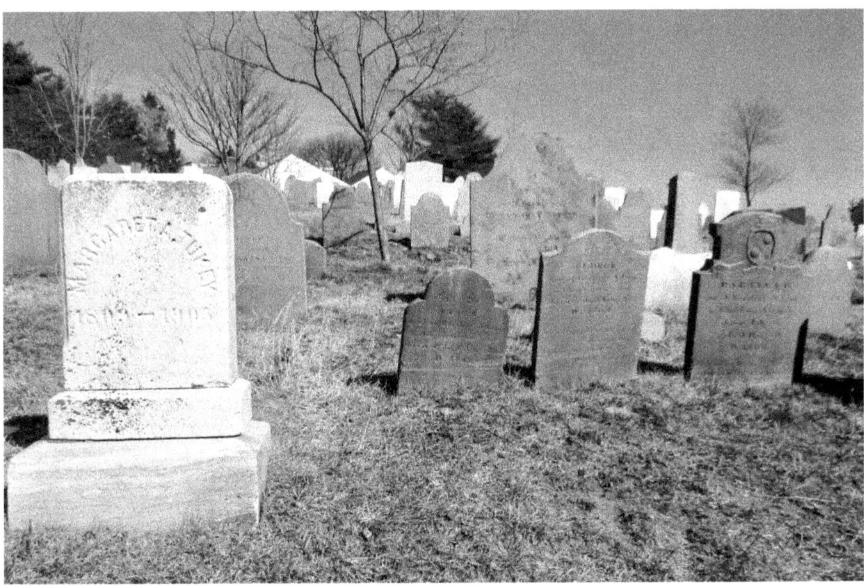

The marble marker for Margaret Tukey, just left of the slates for three of Bartlett Adams's children. Was she actually buried "in George Adams' grave" as her burial note states?

1815, the year his fourth child died. Though the inscribed slab over the tomb is now gone, I assumed that Bartlett had carved the names of all four children on it—even though three were in the open ground nearby—as a way to honor their memory as a family. I thought that perhaps during the 1890 Goodwin survey, the inscribed stone was still intact and the burial records simply reflected that their names appeared both on that stone as well as the individual stones in Section I.

But then I found a record for Margaret Tukey, who passed in 1905, one of the last to be buried at the cemetery. Her burial note reads, "Buried in George Adams' grave. Stone I-203A. [plot number] I-202." George's grave is the middle one, and her stone is just to the left of the three kids. I now believe Bartlett moved his three kids into the tomb around 1815 when his daughter Sarah died. Perhaps he wanted the family together? If true, Tomb A-46 holds Bartlett, Charlotte and six of their children, and Mrs. Tukey has been laid to rest where the three Adams kids originally were buried. Bartlett could very well have decided to leave the three stones standing as a form of advertisement of his ability. The stone for his namesake son is considered to be one of the finest markers he produced in the Portland shop.

PETRIFIED REMAINS

I found the original article in a 1900 *Portland Evening Express* newspaper for an interesting story Jordan included in his book. The article, "Disinterred Petrified Remains," subtitled "Body Buried Forty-Four Years Ago" and "In Perfect State of Preservation," tells the story of the removal of the remains of Captain William Chamberlain to Evergreen Cemetery. He was sailing off the Hawaiian Islands in 1856 when he was killed by an accident aboard his ship. His body was preserved for its return to Portland, as noted by what was discovered at the time of removal:

> *The body of the Captain was placed in a box made of southern pine, three inches thick, and thickly lined with canvas. Around the box were placed large quantities of oakum. In the bottom of the box nearly a barrel of tar was poured. The body was wrapped in canvas, five layers thick, then packed in about 400 pounds of Manila shakings. The voyage home occupied five months. When after 44 years the box was opened...the body was found to be in a perfect state of preservation. The features...looked*

> *as though the Captain had been buried only yesterday. But on touching the body it was found to be hard as stone. In fact the body was petrified.*

Two physicians who attended the disinterment noted that they had never seen a body so petrified, and they attributed the prevention of tissue decay to the particular methods of preservation used to get the body home. Rest in peace, Captain William Chamberlain!

Chapter 15

THREE MONUMENTS AND TWO BOULDERS

Henry A. W. Daniels was unable to survive typhoid fever and died at age seventeen on July 2, 1860. At the time, he was not living with his family; he was at the Maine State Reform School for Boys, the first juvenile detention facility in Maine that had opened just a few years earlier. Henry's death record notes he was "colored," so he was most likely buried in the African American Ground located near the corner of Congress and Mountfort Streets, though no grave marker exists.

James Alden Jr. (1810–1877)

One monument dwarfs all others at Eastern Cemetery. At over twenty feet in height, it's a polished pink granite pedestal honoring Rear Admiral James Alden Jr., a Portland native and direct descendant of *Mayflower* first passengers John Alden and Priscilla Mullins. Alden was born in 1810 and, as a boy, played on the Smith field that would eventually become burial ground. (In fact, historian William Goold wrote that the two played ball together "on the spot where now is his grave.") Like so many native sons, Alden spent his adult life at sea. His naval career began in 1828 at age eighteen. One remarkable voyage lasted four years; in 1838, the U.S. Congress authorized an extensive scientific expedition involving six ships and hundreds of participants. On board were botanists, geologists, biologists and cartographers. (Alden was among the mapmakers.) The fleet explored the South Pacific, charting many islands, and discovered the Antarctic.

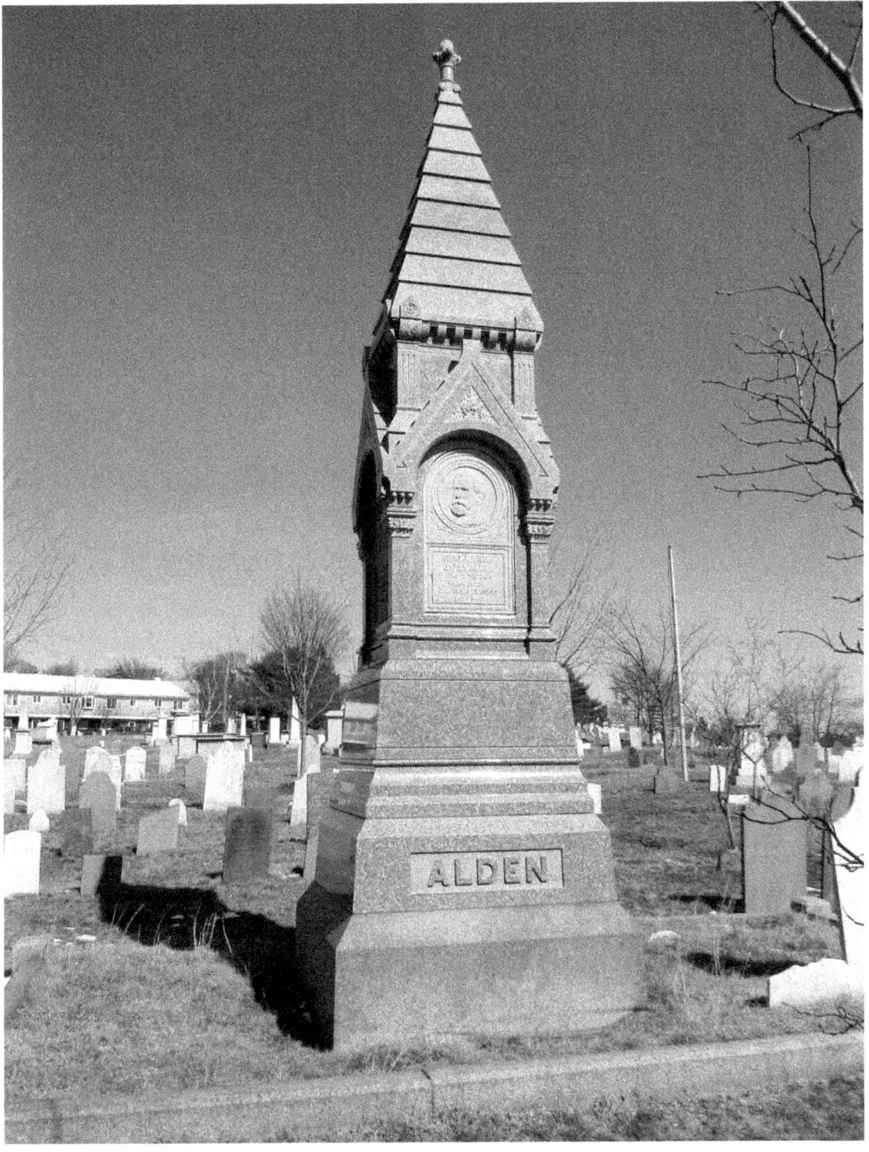

The pink granite monument for Rear Admiral James Alden (1810–1877), the tallest at the cemetery.

Alden later circumnavigated the globe aboard the USS *Constitution* and served in the Civil War. His active service ended when he was sixty-three, and he died four years later in San Francisco. His body was embalmed, allowing transport from the West Coast back home to Portland, where he was laid to

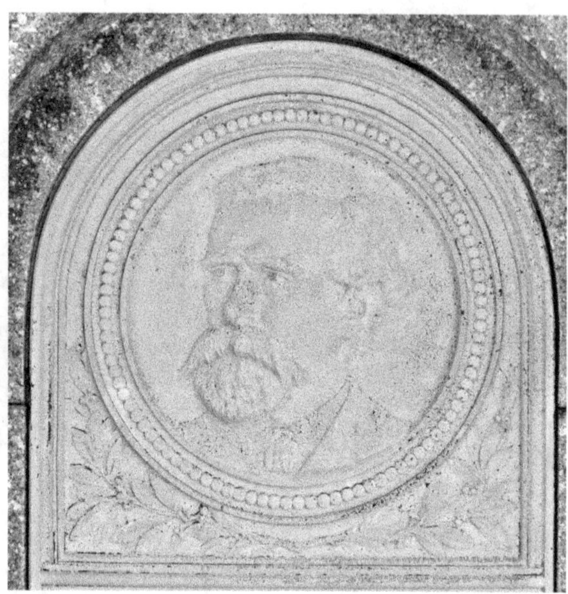

The bronze likeness of Alden from his monument.

rest. Alden was married to Sarah Ann Thompson; no children are known to have been born to them. His monument is adorned with bronze plates depicting his image, dates and service to his country. Also found in his lot are his parents (James Alden and Elizabeth Tate), an infant brother (Benjamin, born and died 1822), his sister (Mary Alden Bradley) and his wife (Sarah Ann Thompson, died in 1889).

Alonzo P. Stinson (1842–1861)

At the front of the cemetery, by the corner of Congress and Mountfort Streets, a large monument was placed in 1908 to honor the first Portland soldier to die in the Civil War. Alonzo P. Stinson was born in 1842. The 1860 U.S. census lists eighteen-year-old Alonzo, the first of seven boys, living with his parents in Auburn, Maine. The next year, at age nineteen, he died on the battlefield at Bull Run, Virginia, just one month into his volunteer service for the Union. He was hit by a cannonball, and though attended to on the battlefield by his younger brother (Harry, age seventeen), he was one of about 800 who died in that conflict. The monument was erected by the survivors of his regiment. The top was carved to feature a soldier's bedroll. Soldiers would keep their personal belongings within the bedroll and carry

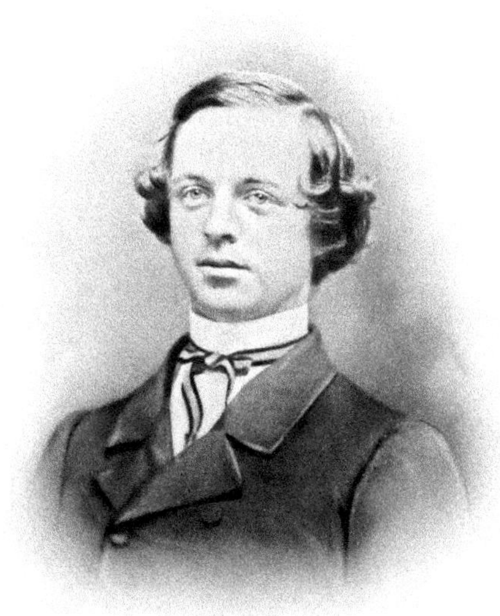

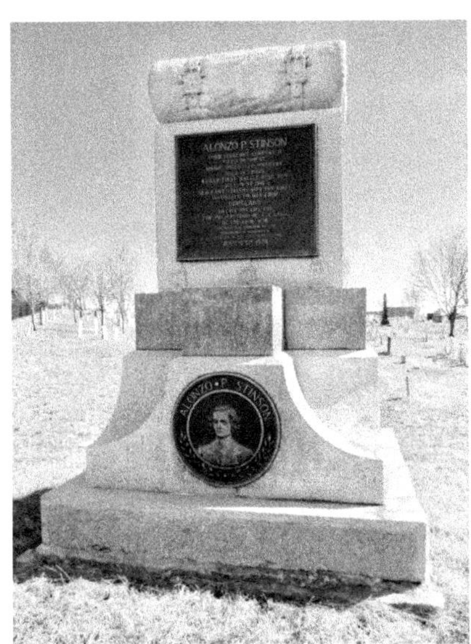

Left: A photo of Alonzo P. Stinson (1842–1861) taken circa 1860. *Collections of Maine Historical Society (www.MaineMemory.net, Item #11502).*

Right: The monument for Stinson, the first Portlander to die in the Civil War. About fifty Civil War veterans are memorialized in the cemetery.

it from one camp to another. Stinson's body was buried near where he died in Virginia, so his monument is a cenotaph. Harry was among the 1,300 captured, and he spent a year in prison. He lived just a few years more after his release. Nearly fifty veterans of the Civil War are memorialized at Eastern Cemetery; the Stinson monument is by far the grandest of them. Note that while the monument was placed within the area considered to be African American burial ground, Stinson was white.

The War of Independence Monument

The third large monument also faces Congress Street but is in the corner next to the old North School. (Built in 1867 after the great fire, it now serves as an apartment building.) This monument was erected in 1909 by the Elizabeth Wadsworth Chapter of the Daughters of the American Revolution. It is a granite obelisk nine feet tall, with a bronze plaque that reads, "To the memory of our historic dead who bore arms in the War

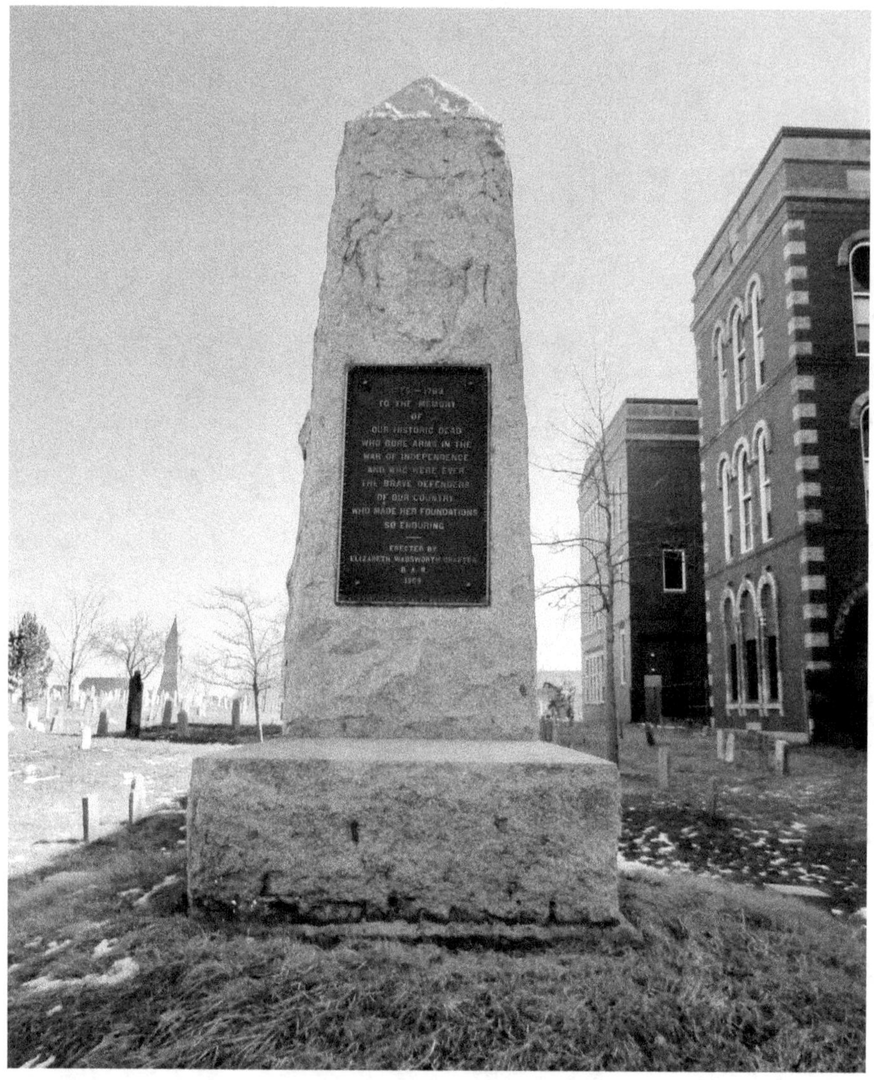

The War of Independence Monument honoring the fifty or more buried in the cemetery who died during service in the American Revolution.

of Independence and who were ever in defense of our city." Frankly, it's a bit understated, and with so much else to see, it is often overlooked. However, it was placed at the cemetery to honor the service of the many veterans who claim Eastern Cemetery as their final resting place. At least fifty veterans of the American Revolution are known to be interred within the cemetery's six acres.

THE BOULDER OPPOSITE THE DEAD HOUSE

One boulder, located on the patch of ground where the Hearse House once stood, provides visitors with a bit of historical context. It was placed by the Longfellow Garden Club in the summer of 1975, soon after the cemetery had been added to the National Register of Historic Places.

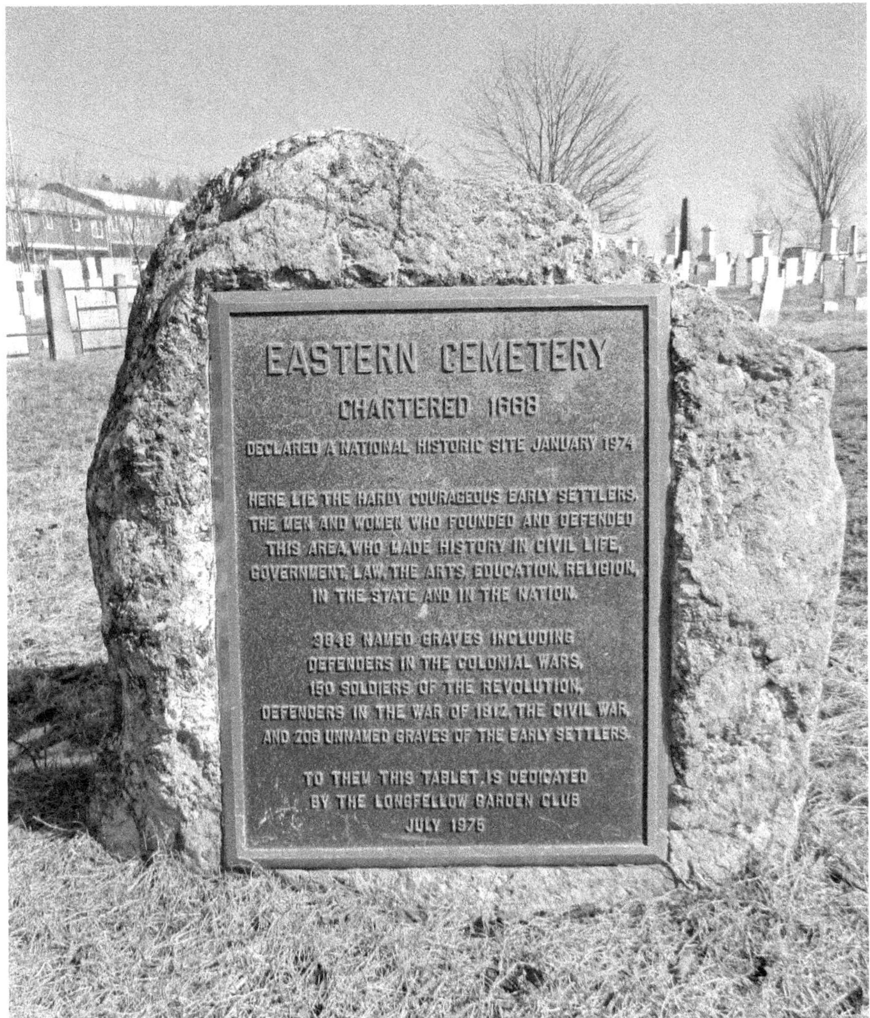

The boulder placed after Eastern Cemetery was added to the National Register of Historic Places.

The Boulder Near the Landmark Pine

The other boulder is found in the old section adjacent to the white pine where the original landmark pine tree grew. It was placed on the 100th anniversary of the War of 1812 and reads:

On this hallowed spot
under the old pine tree
where many of the first
settlers of Portland
were buried,
the National Society
United States Daughters
of 1912 State of Maine
place here this boulder
and tablet in memory of
the brave soldiers and
sailors who served their
country in the War of 1812
and maintained our
independence.
June 1912

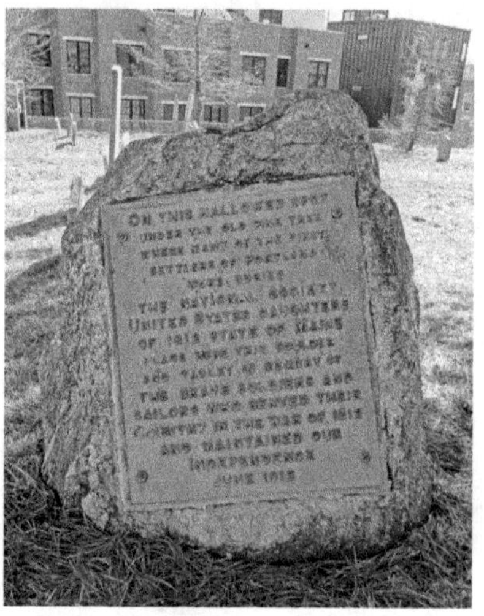

The boulder placed near the landmark pine tree to honor the sixty or more veterans of the War of 1812.

At least sixty veterans of the War of 1812 are known to be interred at Eastern Cemetery.

Chapter 16

THE FAMOUS, IN TWO LINES

Nabby Ford married Lemuel Dyer in Portland in 1812. She was twenty-three; he was twenty-six and working on the wharves as a boat builder. At least three children were born before Nabby died in 1822. She was buried in Tomb A-22 alongside her three-year-old son Robert, who had passed two years earlier. Lemuel wouldn't join them for twenty-five more years, but he did, in 1847 after dying as a result of an accidental injury received while harvesting lumber. His foot was nearly cut in two when hit by an axe from one of his companions.

(In chapter 4, I told of the opening of a tomb to check for structural damage in 2010. That tomb was A-22. During the inspection, two sets of adult human remains were found, one male and one female. These may very well have been Nabby Ford and Lemuel Dyer.)

Thousands of people buried in one historic place brings an equal number of stories. Some are fascinating, others not so much. Some are easily discovered, others require a great deal of research. Some involve heroes, others involve villains. At rest are Portland's mayors, lawyers, judges, preachers, doctors, sea captains and business leaders. But the majority of people buried at Eastern Cemetery were ordinary folk who no doubt worked hard, raised their families and did their best to improve their lives. Listings for children are common; I randomly sampled 315 burial records and found that 86 of those—29 percent of the total—were for children under the age of twelve.

Stories for many of the famous people can be found in other sources. The captains of the HMS *Boxer* (Samuel Blyth) and USS *Enterprise* (William Burrows) from the well-documented battle during the War of 1812 come to mind. Visitors always ask where the oldest stone can be found, but the second most common question is, "Where are the captains?" We always include a stop at the captains' tombs during our tours since their story is so well known. Other people of fame mentioned in preceding chapters include Rear Admiral James Alden, stonecutter Bartlett Adams, early settler Samuel Moody, naval hero Commodore Edward Preble, Civil War casualty Alonzo Stinson and Reverend Thomas Smith.

What follows is a list of selected other people of fame, by year of death, who I summarize in two lines. During tours, our volunteer guides bring visitors to some of these grave sites to tell their stories.

1717: Mary Green holds the honored title of "earliest known gravestone." She was the sister-in-law of Major Samuel Moody, who resettled Portland Neck in 1713.

1777: Tabitha Longfellow and Stephen Longfellow (died 1790), great-grandparents of the poet Henry Wadsworth Longfellow, have markers featuring winged faces that were carved in Boston. The poet is buried in Cambridge, Massachusetts, his parents at Western Cemetery and his grandparents in Gorham, Maine.

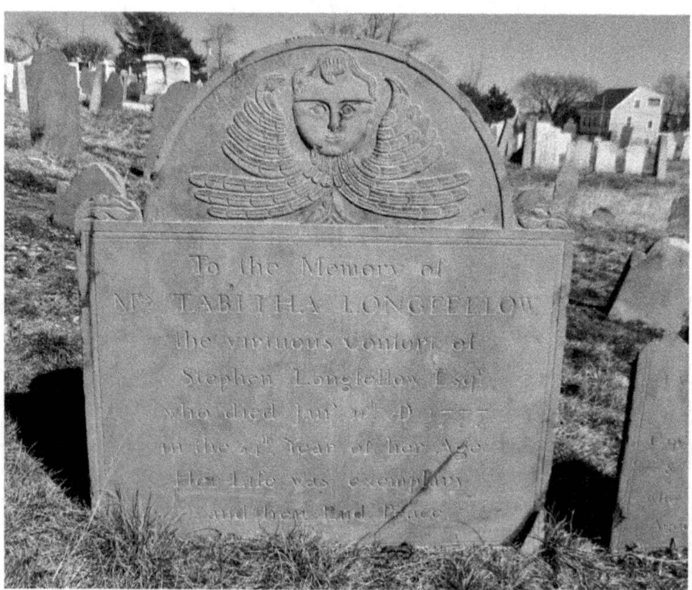

The marker for Tabitha Longfellow, great-grandmother to the poet Henry Wadsworth Longfellow, featuring a winged face by Boston carver Henry Christian Geyer.

1795: Joseph Greenleaf was the first lighthouse keeper of Portland Head Light, having been so assigned that duty by President George Washington. Before downtown development got in the way, his grave—located at the cemetery's highest point—gave visitors a clear view to the lighthouse three miles away.

1804: Lieutenant Henry Wadsworth, uncle to the poet Longfellow, died in Tripoli under the command of Commodore Preble during the Barbary War. His monument had been vandalized and was in pieces on the ground but was brought back to life in 2013.

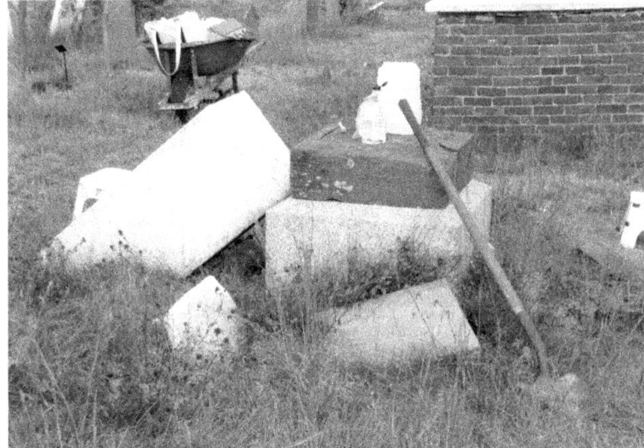

Left: The monument for Lieutenant Henry Wadsworth as found in 2013, toppled by vandals. *Courtesy of Holly Doggett.*

Below: The monument for Lieutenant Henry Wadsworth as found today, after repair.

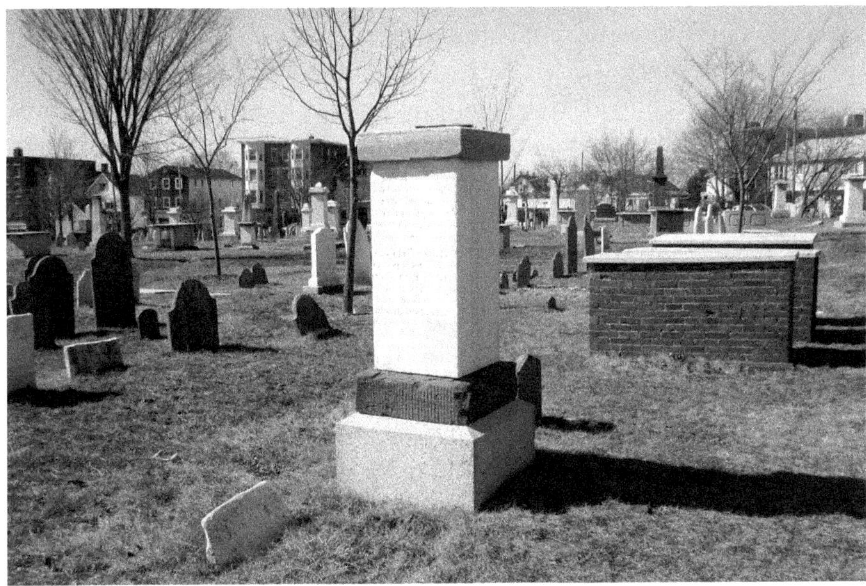

1807: Mary Stonehouse was a wealthy widow from Boston who was drowned, along with her daughter and infant grandson, in the tragic wreck of the schooner *Charles*. Her carved slate at Eastern Cemetery is remarkable for its grand size and voluminous inscription.

1807: Colonel William Tyng was appointed the second sheriff of Cumberland County in 1767 (Moses Pearson was the first) but left the area during the American Revolution. Being loyal to the Crown, he moved to New Brunswick, Canada, to wait out the conflict but returned to Maine in 1793 to live out his final years.

1815: John Russwurm was a wealthy white merchant who impregnated a black Jamaican slave. Their son, John Brown Russwurm, was the second nonwhite person to graduate from an American college (Bowdoin) and became a successful newspaperman and abolitionist.

1833: Elizabeth Phillips delivered at least fourteen children over the course of her fifteen-year marriage, elevating her to fame (in my eyes, anyway). Tragically, all fourteen died in infancy, a sad fact carved onto the slate gravestone made for her when she died at age thirty-eight.

1834: Reverend William Reese was founder of the Widows' Wood Society, supplying fuel to women in need during the cold winters in Portland. His tall marble monument is well placed at the bend in Funeral Lane.

1842: Charles Codman was a talented landscape and marine artist whose works hang in museums throughout the country. His marker was the first and, as it turned out, last one replaced by Spirits Alive, since placing new markers in the historic burial ground is no longer allowed.

1842: George Ropes was an African American conductor of Portland's Underground Railroad. He and his two sons are buried in adjacent graves in the new section of the burial ground, near the designated patch where other African Americans are located.

1846: Lemuel Moody was a sea captain who built the Portland Observatory in 1807. More than forty members of his family are also found at Eastern Cemetery.

1848: Asa Clapp was a successful business leader who became one of the wealthiest men in the state. He loaned half of his personal fortune to the federal government in order to help finance the War of 1812 and then set a wonderful example to the community by enlisting as a private at age fifty. In later years, he hosted two sitting presidents at his home in Portland. (Sorry, that one was three lines.)

1853: Margaret Driver was born a slave in North Carolina in 1769. She and her husband were active in Portland's Union Anti-Slavery Society.

1861: Elizabeth Widgery Thomas was another key player in the antislavery movement in Portland. She owned a safe house near the cemetery and helped enslaved people on their journeys fleeing the South.

Chapter 17

CONSERVATION

Rhoda (Moody) Loring died in 1824 at age thirty-eight and was buried in the new section of the cemetery; her name appears in Jordan's list of interments, and her slate gravestone still stands. Five years later, her husband, Friend Loring, an architect and father of nine children, committed suicide. No burial record or gravestone is known for him, but there is no question that he was buried at Eastern Cemetery, as the October 27, 1829 newspaper reported, "Whereas a rumor has been in circulation, that the grave of Mr. Friend Loring, in the Burying Ground, has been opened and the corpse taken away; This is to certify that we have recently examined said grave, and find that said rumor is without foundation, and that the corpse remains undisturbed." The notice was signed by five men.

Why the rumor existed in the first place is not known. What is known is that two of Mr. Loring's neighbors—George Eaton and another man—spent the night of his burial standing watch over his grave at Eastern Cemetery. Eaton reported that he'd learned of a plan to steal Loring's body and felt compelled to prevent what he viewed as an outrage to the family. In the dark of night, two men came into the cemetery and approached the grave; when Eaton and his companion confronted them, they withdrew. Eaton followed them out and on the way discovered a third man lying in wait for the purpose (he suspected) of carrying Loring's corpse away. We'll probably never know why Friend Loring committed suicide, where he was buried within the cemetery or why his body was nearly stolen from his grave. But thanks to the efforts of his good neighbors so long ago, he rests in peace.

What do time, severe weather, lawn mowers, falling branches, neglect, ground erosion, invasive shrubs and vandalism have in common? They all contribute to the deterioration of early burial grounds. Eastern Cemetery, having been around for more than 350 years, has not escaped any of these threats. Sadly, reports of senseless acts of vandalism at Eastern Cemetery appear in newspapers back to the early 1800s. The Master Plan details ten examples of vandalism—in some cases, widespread destruction of stones—at the cemetery from 1816 through the 1990s, but those are only the accounts reported in the news. Certainly, countless other individual acts have occurred and gone unreported. I know of at least two more instances in 2013 and 2014 involving attempts to break into tombs. Frankly, it's heartbreaking.

But thankfully, Spirits Alive, in partnership with the city, works hard to minimize the risk factors, while restoring the many broken, tipping, lichen-covered grave markers that have survived. Under the leadership of chief conservator Martha Zimicki, volunteers on the Spirits Alive conservation crew do an extraordinary job. The numbers tell the story: in 2013, fifty-two stones were conserved; in 2014, another fifty-two; in 2015, ninety-eight markers conserved; in 2016, seventy-seven more. Nearly three hundred markers have received some tender loving care in four years.

Sometimes the work is relatively easy: a "simple reset" involves carefully digging up the marker, properly preparing the hole it came from and ensuring the stone is replaced straight, level and secure. Other times the work is major: a large marble gravestone broken into three may require the use of a tripod to lift the pieces off the ground, braces to hold the mortared pieces together and careful finish work on the repaired seams to ensure the completed job leaves the stone as close to its original appearance as possible.

Basic conservation requires training, the right equipment, water, some muscle and a desire to improve the sacred ground. Truly successful conservation requires that the individuals doing the work have context about the place where the work is being done. Martha ensures all of us have that context. We use original survey maps to ensure fallen stones are put back exactly where they once stood, we take before and after photographs and we maintain logs of all work done within the cemetery's boundaries. This discipline means that Eastern Cemetery looks better today than it has in decades. On conservation work days, it's not unusual for neighbors from Munjoy Hill to stop by and tell us how fine the grounds look again, and visitors from out of town are full of questions about what we are up to. I always enjoy leading tours during conservation workdays. I bring visitors to

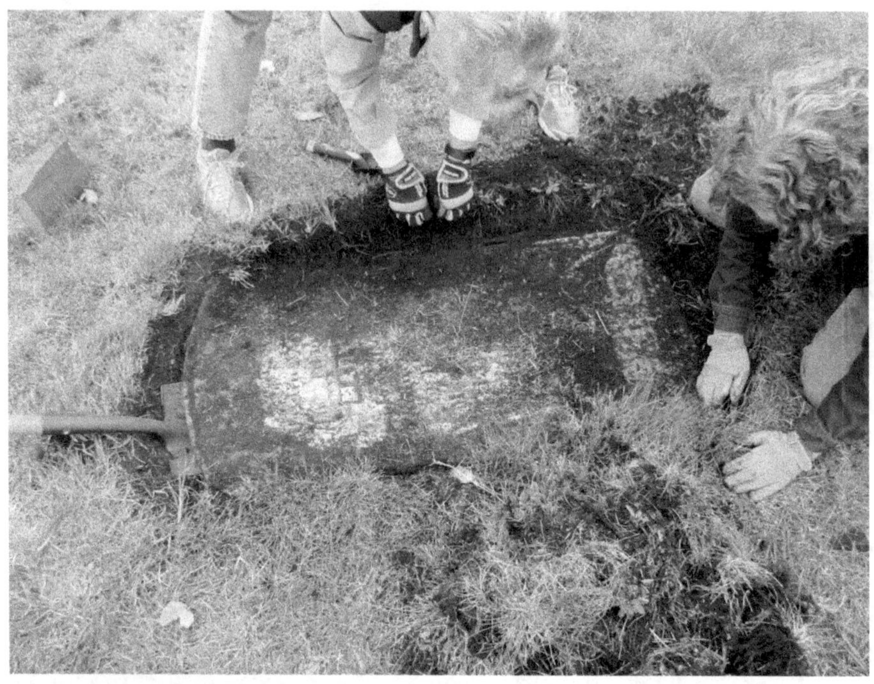

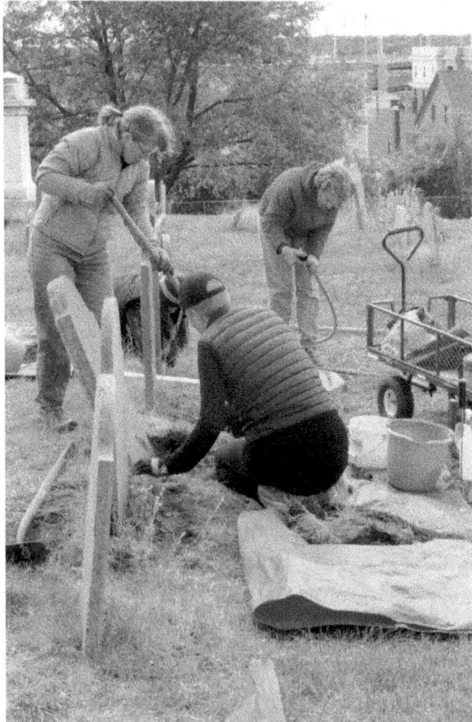

Above: Conservation crew members Janet and Diane unearthing a newly discovered marker.

Left: Martha leads conservation crew members Nikki, Diane and Sarah while aligning a row of markers. *Courtesy of Janet Alexander.*

the worksite so they can see firsthand how their financial support of Spirits Alive helps improve the cemetery.

In recent years, conservation techniques have improved. Mortars and epoxies are now produced that match the colors of stones, helping to minimize the appearance that restorative work has been done. Biologic cleaners have been developed that safely remove and repel lichens and other growth without doing harm to the stone itself. These kinds of advancements aid in the restoration of historic cemeteries, protecting them for future generations.

While the growing interest in the preservation of historic cemeteries has resulted in a more mature, holistic approach to stone conservation, fixing gravestones isn't new. An interesting example is found on two early postcards of Eastern Cemetery in my personal collection. My friend Max Gordon is an avid collector of postcards and was able to narrow down the dates of my cards based on their design details. Both cards are "divided-back," meaning that the writing space on the card is separated into two sides, the left for a personal message and the right for the address. Divided-back postcards without borders were printed between 1907 and 1915; divided-back postcards with narrow white borders were produced from 1915 to 1930.

The subjects of these cards are the brick box tombs for two of our most famous subterranean celebrities, the captains who died in the War of 1812 battle between the *Boxer* and the *Enterprise.* Note the white marble stone just to the left of those tombs. It's the marker for Zaccheus Hannaford, who died in 1835. In the earlier card, Hannaford's stone is broken, but in the later card, we see that it had been repaired. That pinpoints the repair back one hundred years, between 1915 and 1930. Since then, the stone broke again and the remnants are missing or under the sod. The tall bright white marble marker located far left had also broken after the cards were printed, but the Spirits Alive conservation crew repaired and cleaned it during the 2016 conservation cycle.

Cemetery conservation extends beyond stone repair. It also includes landscape work, since falling trees, eroding hillsides and sinkholes all jeopardize the ground. A very steep slope exists in Sections K and L, running east to west about midway through those sections. The slope has more gravel than topsoil and little natural growth. Occasional heavy rains have brought erosion, and many of the early markers on the slope are tilting downward (or have already toppled). In 2015, we targeted that area for conservation. While some of the markers were corrected, our efforts were primarily focused on reseeding the slope with grass in order to prevent

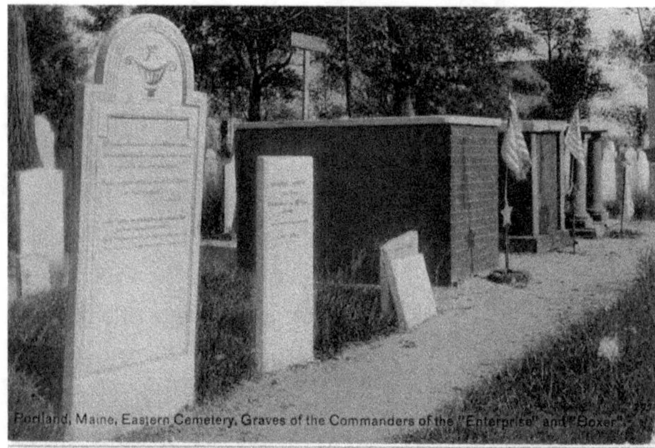

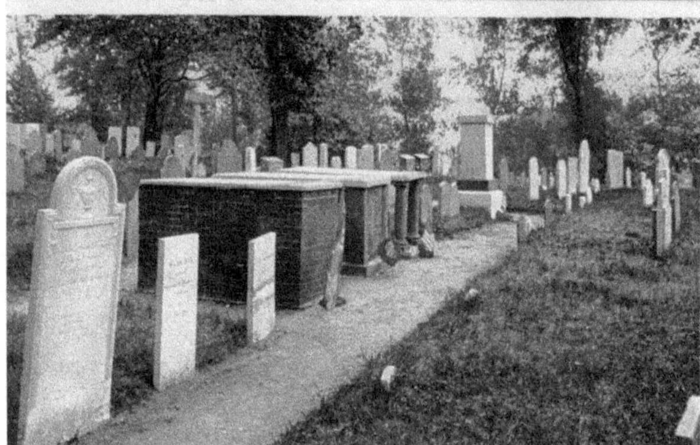

Left: Two postcards of the War of 1812 captains' tombs from the early 1900s. In the older card (*top*), the marble marker to the left of the tombs is broken; in the newer card (*bottom*), it is shown repaired.

Below: Current view of the captains' tombs. In the one hundred years since the postcards were printed, one marble marker left of the tombs has badly broken, and the other has gone missing from view.

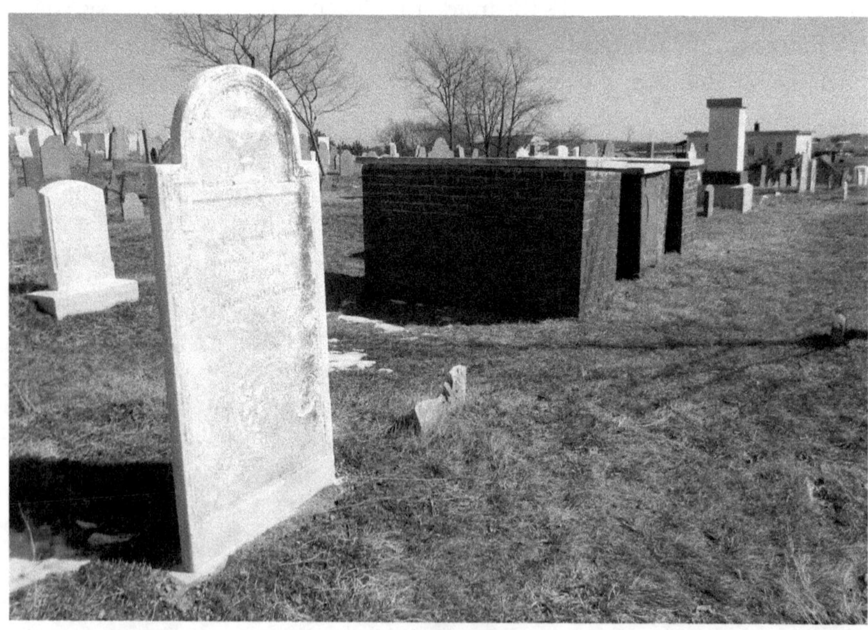

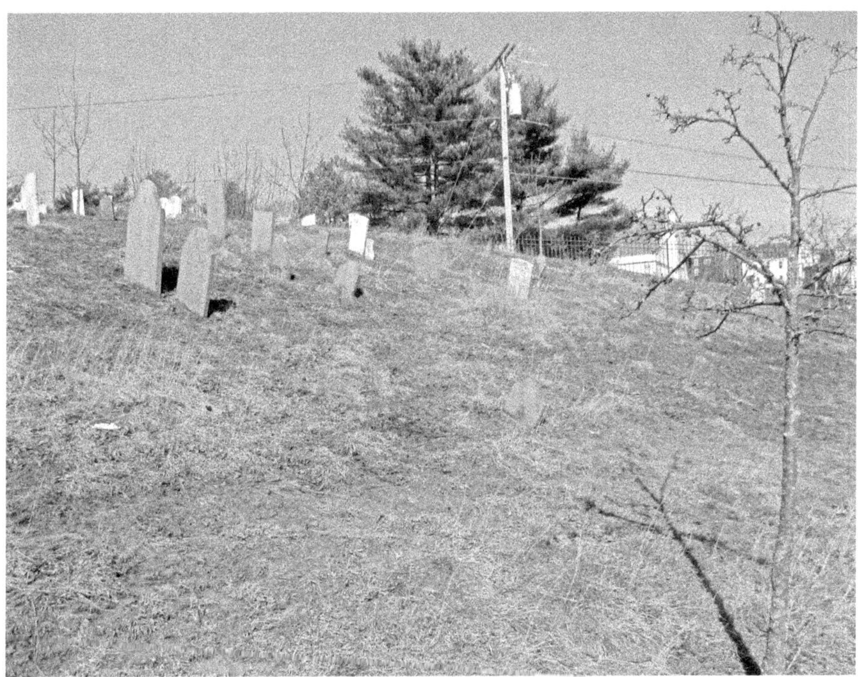

The eroding hillside in Sections K and L. Spirits Alive is straightening the tipping stones and planting grass to minimize further erosion.

further erosion. We measured off a test patch and planted bluestem grass, a native plant, to see if we could improve the situation. Despite frequent watering and careful attention to the test patch, the bluestem did not take to the slope. Though Plan A was unsuccessful, we will develop Plan B and, no doubt, try again.

The Master Plan for Eastern Cemetery notes, "Historic cemeteries are unique and irreplaceable." Eastern Cemetery is just that; it helped shape the history of Portland, it contains as many interesting stories as bodies buried and it deserves our concerted attention so that we don't lose this field of ancient graves forever.

The End

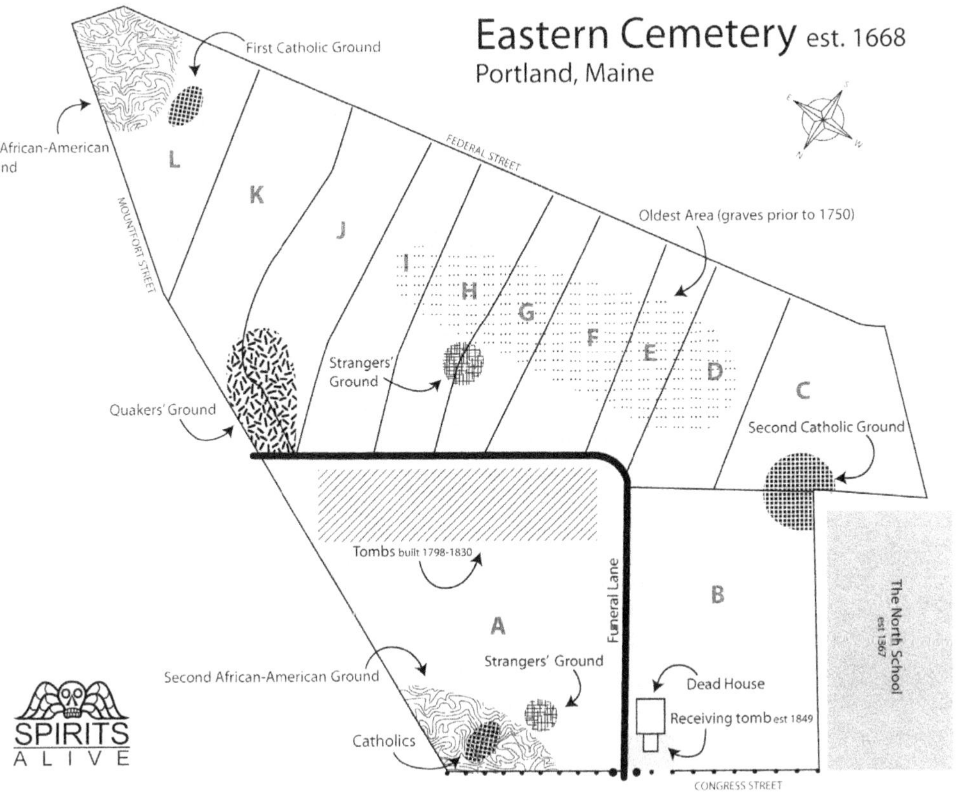

Revised visitors' map showing the designated grounds for African Americans, Quakers, Catholics and strangers. *Courtesy of Diane Brakeley and Spirits Alive.*

Appendix A

TYPES OF MONUMENTS FOUND

Sketches by Holly Doggett

The following three sketches show the types of monuments found at Eastern Cemetery. The first has the most commonly seen slate and marble gravestones, the second has examples of large monuments and the third shows some of the less common and more special markers.

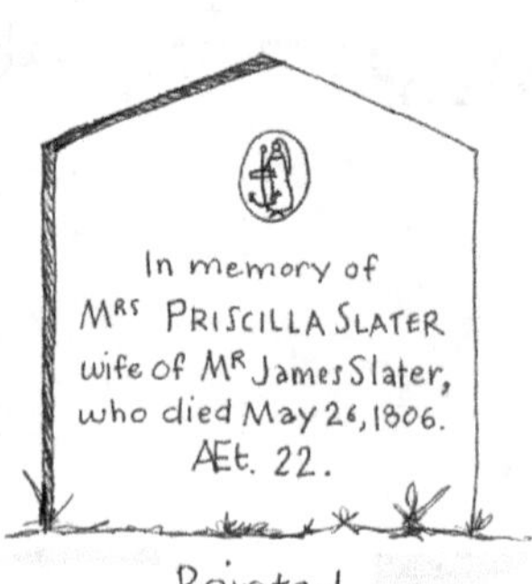

Pointed.

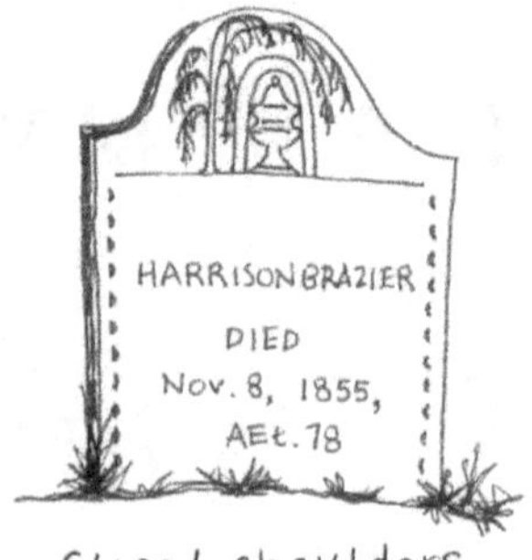

Sloped shoulders.

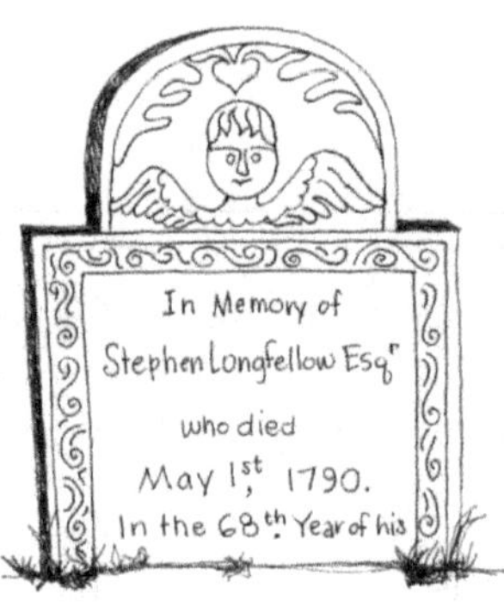

Squared shoulders.

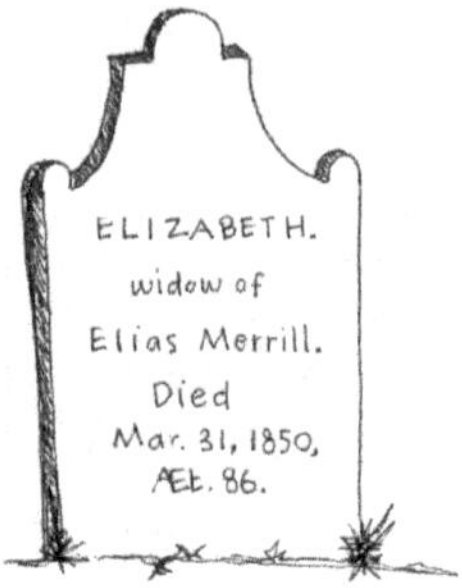

ELIZABETH.
widow of
Elias Merrill.
Died
Mar. 31, 1850,
ÆEt. 86.

Double-shouldered.

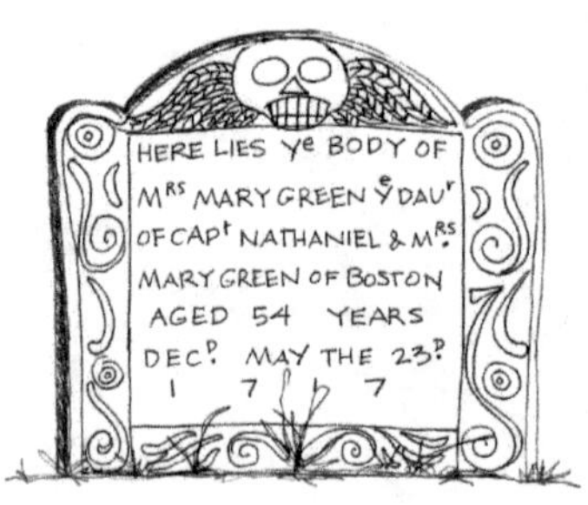

Rounded shoulders.

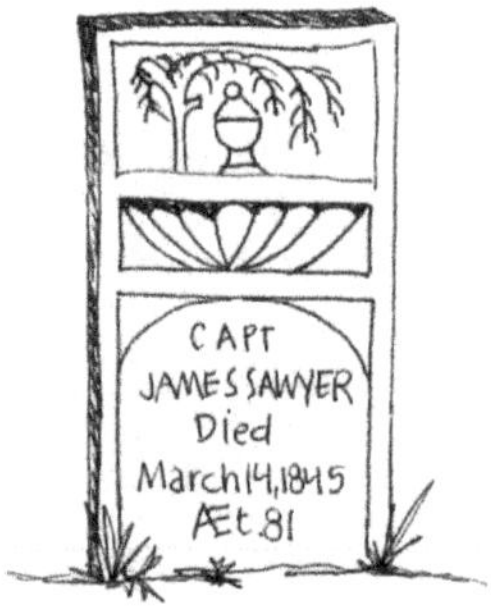

CAPT
JAMES SAWYER
Died
March 14, 1845
ÆEt 81

Squared.

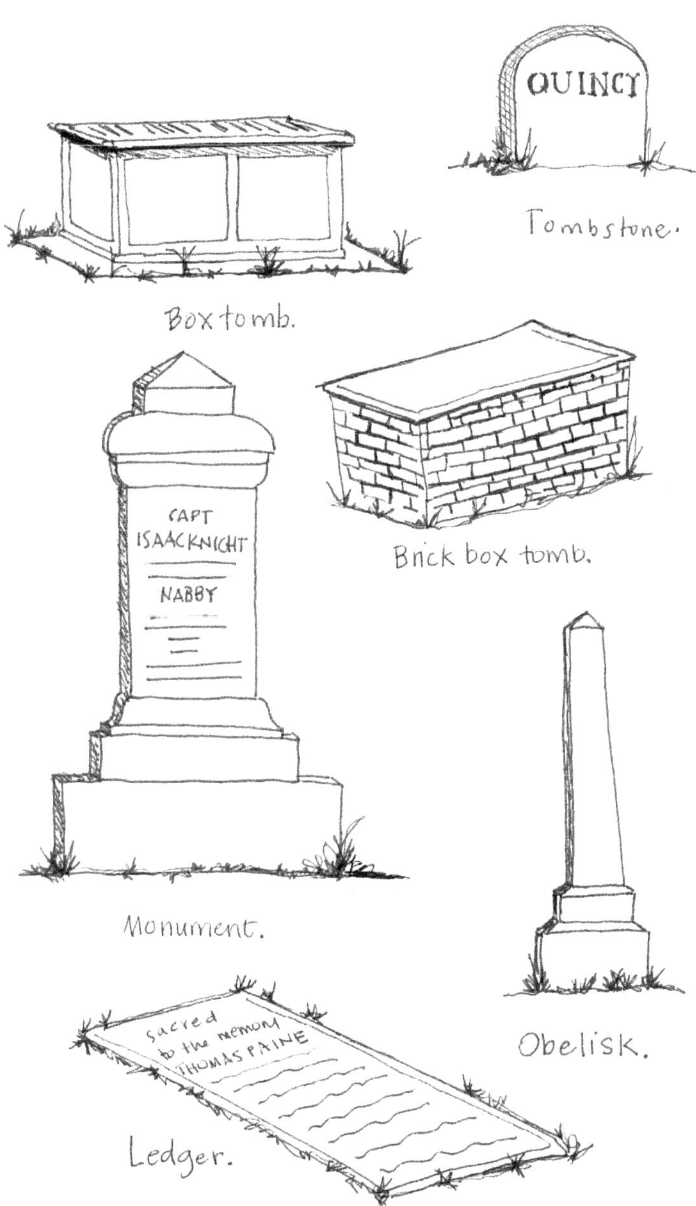
QUINCY
Tombstone.
Box tomb.
CAPT
ISAACKNIGHT
NABBY
Brick box tomb.
Monument.
Obelisk.
sacred
to the memory
THOMAS PAINE
Ledger.

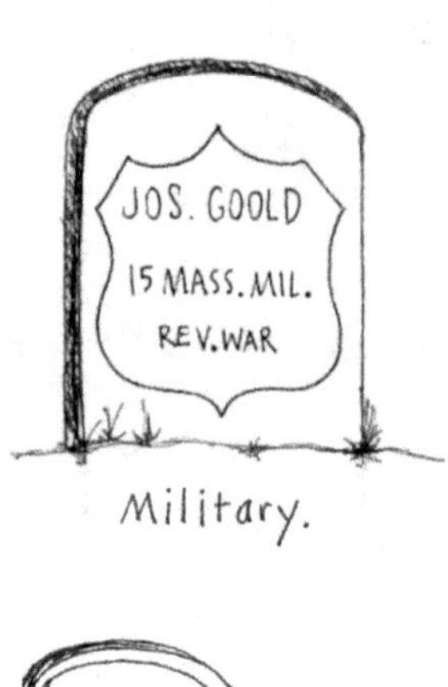

Military.

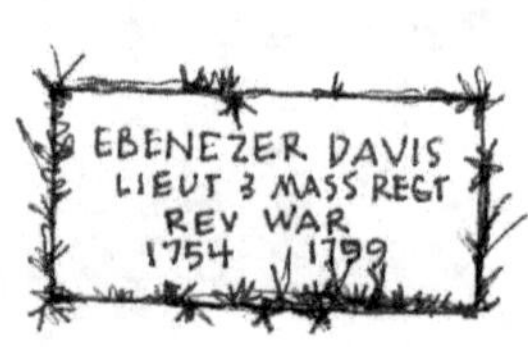

Flat military.

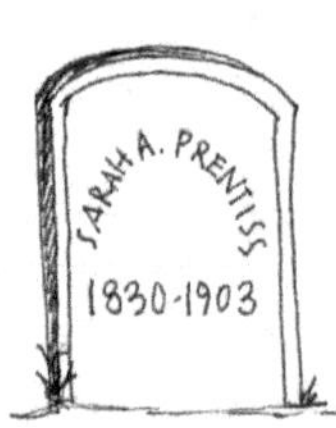

Rounded.

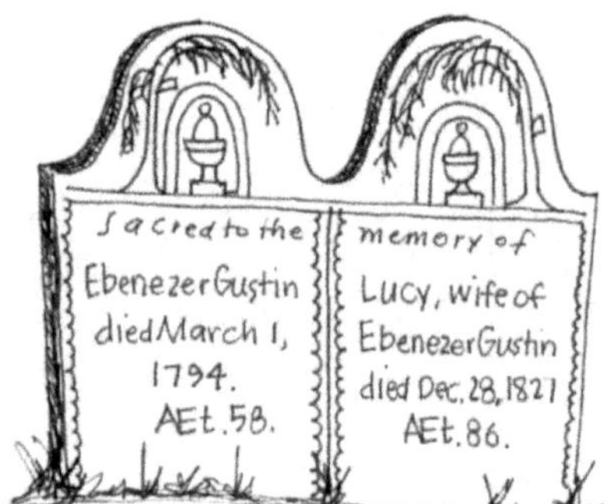

Double timpanum.

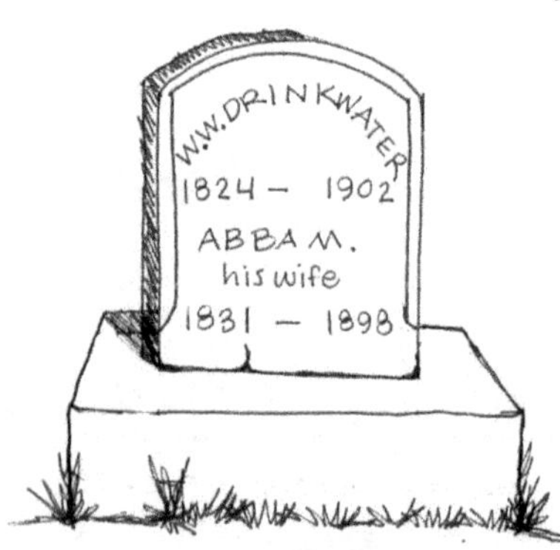

Pinned to base.

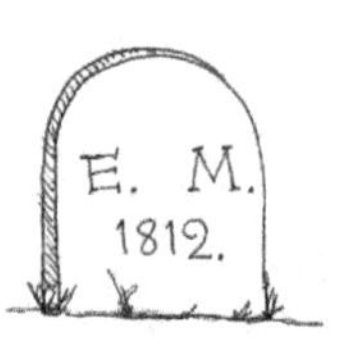

Footstone.

Appendix B

GRAVESTONE SYMBOLISM, WORDS AND ABBREVIATIONS

The following are found on grave markers at Eastern Cemetery. Regular type indicates symbols; bold, italic style indicates words and abbreviations. See the *Association for Gravestone Studies* Field Guide #8 and the *Maine Old Cemetery Association* website for more.

Symbol, Word or Abbreviation	**Use and/or Meaning**
"AE" or "AEt"	***Latin for* aetatis suae*, meaning "at the age of."***
anchor	Decoration for sea captains; also symbolizes hope.
angel (full figure), flying	Rebirth, or the messenger between the living and God. Much more common are Winged Faces (see "face").
baby	Decoration for infants, represents eternal sleep.
Bible	Decoration for a deeply religious person, signifies faith.
bird, dove	Usually a dove, sometimes carrying a branch, these are messengers of peace and innocence.

Symbol, Word or Abbreviation	Use and/or Meaning
bones	Usually carved as two crossed bones, these represent the finality of death, a reminder that all must die (see "skull").
book	Likely a Bible, the decoration for a deeply religious person, signifies faith.
broken tree branch	Frequently found on weeping willow trees, signifies a life cut short.
chain links	Usually with letters, used on gravestones for members of the Odd Fellows organization.
cherub	(see "face")
columns	A pair of columns signifies passage from the known to unknown worlds; a single column represents strength.
compass and square	Often decorating grave markers for freemasons.
"Consort"	***A woman whose death has preceded her husband's.***
cross and crown	Resurrection; triumph over death.
Cross, Holy	Found on markers for Catholics, symbolizes religious faith and resurrection.
curtain, drapery	Passage from one realm to the next.
death's head	(see "skull")
"Esq."	***Short for Esquire, meaning a lawyer.***
face, winged	Represents the flight of the soul to heaven. Some call these cherubs or angels, but those are typically full figures with wings emerging from their backs.
finger pointing upward	Gone home, departed, no longer on earth.
flame	Eternity.

Symbol, Word or Abbreviation	**Use and/or Meaning**
flowers	Often on gravestones for children or women, these represent the frailty of life and the innocence of children. A poppy represents eternal sleep; a rose represents beauty. Broken flower buds represent a life cut short.
globe, orb	Symbol of creation, reward of resurrection.
hands, clasped	Sometimes on a marker for a husband or wife, honors the relationship between the one who is living and the other who has passed.
heart	Love, or love of Christ (on Catholic markers).
heart, upside-down	Unknown meaning.
"Hine lachrymis"	***Latin for "hence these tears."***
hourglass	The passage of time, the brevity of life.
"I.II.S."	***Latin for* Iesus hominum salvatore, *meaning "Jesus, the savior of humankind." Sometimes spoken as "In his service."***
lamb	Innocence of a child.
"Memento Mori"	***Latin for "remember you must die."***
"Memoria Sacrum"	***Latin for "in sacred memory."***
"M.S."	***Latin abbreviation for* Memoria Sacrum, *or "in sacred memory."***
"Ob.," "Obt." or "Obit."	***Latin abbreviations for "he/she died on... (date of death)."***
obelisk	Greatness, patriotism.
palm fronds	Usually crossed, represents spiritual victory over death.
pinwheel (and other geometric designs)	These are artistic space-fillers more than meaningful symbols.
"Relict"	***A woman whose death follows her husband's.***

Symbol, Word or Abbreviation	Use and/or Meaning
scroll	Religious scripture and the Bible; the unfurling of life.
scythe	The tool of the Grim Reaper, divine harvest, reaping of life.
shield	Often used on military markers.
ship	Decoration for sea captains.
skull, winged	The skull represents the mortal remains, and the wings represent the flight of the soul to heaven. Some call these "death's heads."
skull with bones	Finality of death.
starburst	Found decorating many urns on stones at Eastern Cemetery; likely only a decorative element.
sun	Rising sun represents resurrection, renewed life. Some consider these setting suns, representing the end of life. At Eastern Cemetery, all of the dozen rising suns were carved in the Bartlett Adams shop and were personified with eyes, eyebrows and hair.
tree	Life. Most commonly found are weeping willows, which have special meaning (see "weeping willow").
umbrella	Unknown meaning.
urn	Represents death; paired with a weeping willow, it's the most common design found.
vines	Religious faith.
weeping willow	Represents mourning, grief, sorrow; paired with an urn, it's the most common design found.
wreath	Spiritual victory over death.

Appendix C

POSTSCRIPTS FOR *EARLY GRAVESTONES IN SOUTHERN MAINE*

Since the publication of *Early Gravestones*..., a few discoveries have been made. Here are updates on Bartlett's two nephews, each of whom took over Bartlett's shop temporarily, and a note about signed markers.

Alvan Washburn

I ended the chapter on this nephew with "Very little else is known about Alvan Washburn. No records are found of a marriage or children, his whereabouts during U.S. census years or a date or location of his death...By 1820, he seems to have simply vanished into thin air."

I've since discovered later records using "Alvin" that had initially thrown me off course. Once Alvan left his uncle's shop around 1815, he moved to Ohio. There, he married Margaret Noble and opened a stone shop. He focused more on cutting stone for construction rather than gravestones. In 1826, he received recognition in a Cincinnati journal for developing a steam-powered mill for sawing large blocks of construction stone. He had no children. He lived a full life, passing in 1868 at the age of seventy-six; a monument is found today on his grave in Lynchburg, Ohio.

Appendix C

Elias Washburn

My chapter on Alvan's younger brother focused on his sloppy carving style. His inattention to detail—especially in his earlier years of carving—resulted in a collection of about one hundred markers in Maine, most with a distinctive lack of finesse. I discovered more about him, leading me to title a presentation at an Association for Gravestone Studies meeting "The Bad Boy Stonecutter." Not only was his carving below his uncle Bartlett's standards, but Elias also had some personal baggage. His move to Maine at age twenty-one likely wasn't just about helping his uncle at the shop. In May 1817, he was in Massachusetts, engaged to fifteen-year-old Lydia Allen. Within a month, they were married and moved to Maine. By November, Lydia delivered their first child. It had been, to use a Maine expression, a "wicked short" pregnancy, and it explains the speedy marriage and move out of town. Convenient was Portland and work in his uncle's shop. However, all is not well that ends well, for I discovered a notice in an 1822 newspaper in which Bartlett announced that due to Elias's refusal to honor the terms of their working agreement, he was declaring it invalid. Something must have happened between them to cause this awkward end. Elias returned to Massachusetts, but he died at age thirty, leaving Lydia and their children behind.

Signed Markers

Finding a carver signature on a marker is an "aha moment," since signatures help us learn the carving style of the individual stonecutters. But signed markers are rare. Before about 1850, if a carver did sign his work, the signature was below ground. While some of Eastern Cemetery's Boston-era stones (that is, pre-1800) may have been signed by their carvers, we don't know of any. During Bartlett Adams's time in Portland (1800–28), he did not sign his markers. But while doing some simple resets and cleanings, we have found below-ground initials from Alvan and Elias Washburn on about a dozen of their slates.

By 1850, more carvers were in town, and competition among them led some to sign their work. Post-1850 signatures are almost always above ground and likely served as a form of advertising. Since Eastern Cemetery has so few markers from the second half of the 1800s, signatures are

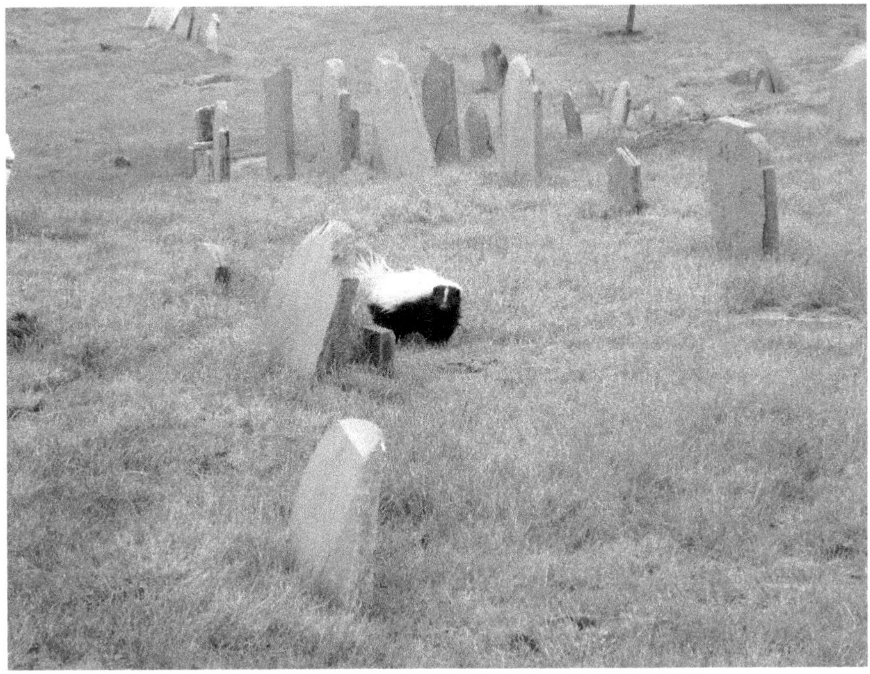

Eastern Cemetery's unofficial mascot.

scarce. But at least six signed stones exist from local mid-century carvers: four from the shop of Henry Hanson, one from William H.H. Merrill and one from the shop of John Hunt & James Jewett.

BIBLIOGRAPHY

Bannatyne, James. *Intemperance Among Literary Men, An Address.* Portland, ME: A. Shirley and Son, Printers, 1842.

Barker, Matthew Jude. *The Irish of Portland, Maine: A History of Forest City Hibernians.* Charleston, SC: The History Press, 2014.

Blachowicz, James. *From Slate to Marble.* Vol. 1. Evanston, IL: Graver Press, 2006.

———. *From Slate to Marble.* Vol. 2. Evanston, IL: Graver Press, 2015.

Bruce, Noah. "Maine History X." *Portland Phoenix*, August 30–September 6, 2001.

Buker, George E. *Swamp Sailors: Riverine Warfare in the Everglades 1835–1842.* Gainesville: University Press of Florida, 1975.

Clayton, W. Woodford. *History of Cumberland Co., Maine.* Philadelphia: Everts & Peck, 1880.

Colesworthy, D.C. *Chronicles of Casco Bay.* Portland, ME: Sanborn and Carter (Press of A. Shirley and Son), 1850.

Cumberland County Justice of the Peace Records. Maine Historical Society, 1982.

Drake, B., and E.D. Mansfield. *Cincinnati in 1826.* Cincinnati, OH: Morgan, Lodge & Fisher, 1827.

Drake, Samuel Adams. *The Pine Tree Coast.* Boston: Estes & Lauriat, 1891.

Ellms, Charles. *The Tragedy of the Seas.* New York: Israel Post, 1841.

Elwell, Edward H. *Portland and Vicinity.* Portland, ME: Greater Portland Landmarks, 1975. (Originally published 1876, revised 1881.)

Forbes, Harriette Merrifield. *Gravestones of Early New England and the Men Who Made Them, 1653–1800.* Boston: Riverside Press/Houghton Mifflin, 1927.

Genesio, Jerry. *Portland Neck*. Lexington, KY, 2013.

Giguere, Joy M. "Death and Commemoration on the Frontier: An Archeological Analysis of Early Gravestones in Cumberland County, Maine." Master's thesis, University of Maine, 2005.

Goold, William. *Portland in the Past*. Portland, ME: B. Thurston & Company Publishers, 1886.

Gould, William E. "Portland Banks." *Collections and Proceedings of the Maine Historical Society*. Second Series, vol. 4. Portland, ME: published by the Society, 1893.

Grannell, Andrew, comp./trans. *Chronology of Maine Friends Meetings with Focus on Forest Avenue Friends Meeting*. N.p., 2017.

Hearn, Daniel Allen. *Legal Executions in New England: A Comprehensive Reference, 1623–1960*. Jefferson, NC: McFarland & Company Inc., 1999.

Hoadley, William F. *Inscriptions in the old Eastern Cemetery, Portland, Maine.* Archival Collections #861 at Maine Historical Society, 1897.

Homans, B., ed. *The Army and Navy Chronicle.* Vol. 8, *From January 1 to June 30, 1839*. Washington, D.C.: B. Homans, 1839.

Irish Americans Buried in Eastern Cemetery and Western Cemetery, Portland, Maine. Archival Collections #S-6672 at Maine Historical Society, circa 2000.

Jordan, William B., Jr. *Burial Records, 1717–1962, of the Eastern Cemetery, Portland, Maine.* Westminster, MD: Heritage Books, 1987.

———. *Record of Interments with Historical Notes (Eastern Cemetery)*. Maine Historical Society Collections, 1978.

Ledman, Paul J. *Walking Through History: Portland, Maine on Foot.* Portland, ME: Next Steps Publishing, 2016.

Levinsky, Allan. *A Short History of Portland.* N.p.: Applewood Books, 2007.

Master Plan for Eastern Cemetery, City of Portland, Maine. Columbia, SC: Chicora Foundation Inc., 2011.

McLellan, Hugh D. *History of Gorham, ME*. Portland, ME: Smith and Sale, Printers, 1903.

Moulton, Augustus F. *Portland by the Sea*. Augusta, ME: Katahden Publishing Company, 1926.

Niles' National Register. Vol. 5, September 1838–March 1839.

Peopling Maine. Maine History Online, Maine Historical Society.

Portland. Portland, ME: Greater Portland Landmarks, 1972.

Portland City Guide. Portland, ME: Forest City Printing Company, 1940.

Portland Freedom Trail. Self-guided walking tour brochure.

The Railway Conductor 19, no. 1. "The Passing of Deep-Sea Mutinies." January 1912.

Robinson, J. Dennis. *Mystery on the Isles of Shoals: Closing the Case on the Smuttynose Ax Murders of 1873*. New York: Skyhorse Publishing, 2014.

Romano, Ron. *Early Gravestones in Southern Maine: The Genius of Bartlett Adams.* Charleston, SC: The History Press, 2016.

Snodgrass, Mary Ellen. *The Underground Railroad: An Encyclopedia of People, Places, and Operations.* N.p.: Routledge Publishing, 2008.

South Australian Advertiser, December 9, 1858.

Symbolism in the Carvings on Old Gravestones. AGS Field Guide #8. Greenfield, MA: Association for Gravestone Studies, 2012.

Watson, S.M., Esq., comp. *Tombstone Inscriptions in Eastern Cemetery, Portland, Maine.* Archival Collections #S-1227, Maine Historical Society.

Willis, William. *The History of Portland.* Facsimile edition of original publication of 1865 for Maine Historical Society. Somersworth: New Hampshire Publishing Company, 1972.

———. *Journals of the Rev. Thomas Smith and the Rev. Samuel Deane, Pastors of the First Church of Portland.* Portland, ME: Joseph S. Bailey Publishing Company, 1849.

Yates, Octavius K. "Last Words of Peter Williams and Abraham Cox." Broadside, 1858.

Yetter, Luann. *Portland's Past.* Charleston, SC: The History Press, 2011.

Websites and General References

ancestry.com (family trees and other vital records)
BeautyinDeath.com (Quaker burial practices)
bidderfordpoolmaine.com (Lowell accident)
cjrc.osu.edu (hangings)
Collections at Boston Public Library
Collections at Maine Historical Society
cumberlandso.org (hanging of Drew)
deathpenaltyusa.org/usa1/state/maine (hangings)
Eastern Argus newspaper
findagrave.com
genealogy.com (Anne Taber biographical sketch)
graveaddiction.com (symbolism)
historicalcharts.noaa.gov
Maine Birth Records, 1621–1922
Maine Death Records, 1617–1922

maine.gov (Maine Civil War Monuments)
MaineIrishHeritageTrail.org (Catholics)
Maine Marriage Records, 1713–1937
milhomme.blogspot.com (Catholics)
Portland Gazette newspaper
Portland, Maine Directories
Portland Transcript newspaper
quakerspeak.com (Quaker burial practices)
SoMeOldNews.com (Lowell accident)
StrangeMaine.blogspot.com (hangings of Williams and Cox)
U.S. Federal Census Records, 1790–1940

INDEX

G

H

M

O

P

Q

R

S

T

U

W

ABOUT THE AUTHOR

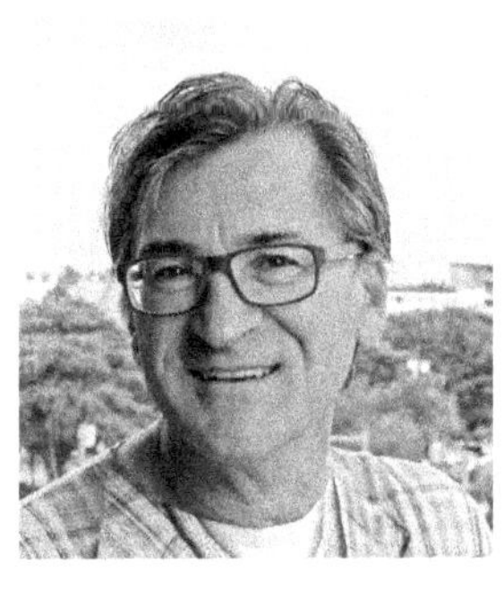

Courtesy of JoAnne Russo.

A native of Portland, Maine, Ron Romano spent his college and career years in Boston, returning to his hometown in 2011. He serves on the board of Spirits Alive—the Friends of Portland's Eastern Cemetery—leading their walking tours program, participating in stone conservation and researching gravestones and their makers at the historic burial ground. Ron is a frequent lecturer on the early stonecutters of southern Maine and has guided groups through many historic cemeteries in the area. His original research on the life and work of stonecutter Bartlett Adams led to the publication of his first book in 2016. Ron winters in south Florida, and since no good colonial cemeteries are there to explore, he enjoys tropical bird-watching. He has *not* yet found a flamingo in the wild.

Visit us at
www.historypress.net

This title is also available as an e-book

www.ingramcontent.com/pod-product-compliance
Lightning Source LLC
LaVergne TN
LVHW010938100826
845153LV00001B/79

9781540227140